MEN
VOID
OF LIGHT

To: Sam

You Were Made in the Image and the
Likeness of The Most High God to
Manifest His Glorious Light- So Continue
to Shine bright.

Agape Shalom

Fidel M. Donaldson

MEN VOID OF LIGHT:

Father, Where Are You?

FIDEL DONALDSON

WRITERS INCARCERATED
PUBLISHING

"unlock your dreams"

Writers Incarcerated Publishing
Los Angeles, California

MEN VOID OF LIGHT: FATHER, WHERE ARE YOU?
ISBN: 978-0-578-29387-5
Copyright © 2022 by Fidel Donaldson
Published by: Writers Incarcerated Publishing
4859 W Slausen Ave, Unit A # 223, Los Angeles CA 90056

Edited by Rebekah J. Sawyer
Cover Design by Christopher C. White
Interior Design by Reider Books

This book is dedicated to Yahshua, the Light of the World, and to every man who makes a conscious decision to be a bearer and witness of His Light.

ACKNOWLEDGEMENTS

I would like to express my heartfelt thanks and gratitude to the selfless individuals who took time out of their busy schedules to guide me through the process of writing this book: to my friend and mentor, Mr. Laval Belle; to the great woman Apostle, Teresa Rena Vaughn Ball; and last but certainly not least, to my brother Patrice Donaldson, A.K.A. Lenky, and to all Christian Soldiers bearing witness of the Light behind the walls. It was behind the walls where I first encountered the Light of the World, so I am always motivated and inspired to write to that captive, yet free, audience.

To the gifted, talented people at Writers Incarcerated Publishing, I owe a debt of gratitude to you for your diligence and your excellent approach to publishing.

CONTENTS

FOREWORD

Then God said, "Let there be light." When God said, "Let there be light," He clearly implied there was darkness. At the time of creation, planet earth was in cosmic chaos and devoid of order. The first order of business in that divine construction process was providing light. Light is simply the absence of darkness. Then what is darkness?

Darkness is a necessary ingredient in the process of light. You cannot have a complete day without darkness. The first man God created was a man of color. Every child born of the seed of man travels through the dark womb of a woman.

Light, on the other hand, is illumination. Light represents freedom, inspiration, and divine destiny. However, oftentimes as men we are overwhelmed with the confusion and impact of negative, dark forces. The negative circumstances of darkness don't define us as men, but they can develop us as men. Muhammed Ali's pain and physical setbacks didn't impede him from carrying and lighting the Olympic torch during the opening ceremony of the 1996 Centennial Olympic Games.

Fidel Donaldson, a native of Jamaica, West Indies, is a living example of how God transformed his negative, dark circumstances into opportunities and tools of freedom. When he was five years of age, Fidel's mother, Monica Maxwell, decided to relocate her family to America to escape the violent, impoverished inner city of Kingston, Jamaica. While growing up in Brooklyn, NY,

Donaldson experienced many of the dark elements of America's streets. He experienced molestation, racism, police brutality, bullying, and unbearable hardships.

Like many youths, and particularly African American males, Fidel turned to a lifestyle of drugs and crime for survival. That decision landed him in prison in England, an entire continent away from home. *Crime will take you farther than you want to go, keep you longer than you want to stay; crime will cost you more than you want to pay!*

From the words of fellow Jamaican recording artist Papa San, "Ignorance is a deadly disease." But it was there in the dark prison of England where Fidel Donaldson came face to face with the light of truth, the light of healing, and the light of manhood. Donaldson encountered the light of his Father God and discovered his true purpose as a messenger of hope and freedom.

Fidel's journey brought him full circle. In Jamaica, while speaking at a tent revival, he noticed many of the young males posed in a posture of doubt and skepticism. As he continued his message, he began to share his own life story. As a result of his transparency, the young men went from a posture of doubt and skepticism to receptive ears and open hearts. They came forward seeking the transformative light of God.

In his book, *"Men Void of Light: Father Where Are You?"* Fidel Donaldson shares the life-changing story of his experiences as a youth searching for guidance, a father, and manhood. His transformation experience will revolutionize every reader. You will discover the light of God, the light of male affection, and the light of fatherhood. Brother, that light is you.

-Laval Belle
Minister, and Author of, "Your Gifts Are Not Your Purpose"

INTRODUCTION

W hat is a void? As an adjective it means, "completely empty." As a noun it means, "a completely empty space." I believe a void—an empty space—was left in the heart of the original man when rebellion caused him to be disconnected from his Creator. The darkness which entered the void in his heart made him capable of the most heinous acts. Its tentacles negatively impact every man—why? Because all men trace their lineage, their genealogy, through him. Here is the solution: the darkness must be replaced with light. Only one kind of light can accomplish this herculean feat—it is the Light which comes from the Father of Lights. Apostle James said this about Him, *"With whom is no variableness, neither shadow of turning"* (Jas. 1:17).

In 2019, I received a mandate and an assignment which propelled me to embark on a journey to write this book during a tent revival in Jamaica, West Indies, in a community called Hatfield, in the parish of Manchester. I made what I considered to be a very important observation. Several men in the service were aloof and disconnected. As my eyes perused the audience, my heart was stirred to do something about the lethargy I witnessed in some of the men and a scripture came to my mind:

There was a man sent from God, whose name was John. The same came for a witness, to bear witness of the Light, that all

men through him might believe. He was not that Light but was
sent to bear witness of that Light.—John 1:6-8

Upon my return home, I started typing the manuscript that
would become this book. I worked diligently on it because I felt
the weight of the importance of the subject matter. If one man,
John, was given the assignment to bear witness of the Light so all
men could believe, I could do my part to bring wisdom, knowledge, and understanding to as many men I could reach. The pen is
mightier than the sword, and a book can be sent to places—especially electronically—where I may not be able to reach.

My hope is that this book would motivate, encourage, and
inspire men to bear witness of the Light—to be an example, not
only to other men, but also to women and children.

CHAPTER 1

THE VOID

A life without God is a tragic voyage on Earth,
because in life there is a certain void that only God can fill.
—*Gift Gugu Mona, "Daily Quotes about God:*
365 Days of Heavenly Inspiration"

Man that is born of a woman is of few days and full of trouble.
—*Job 14:1*

THE PROBLEM

Every man born into the earth through the matrix of a woman, conceived in her womb by a father's sperm, came into this realm with a void—a vacant place in his soul desperately in need of something to fill it. He can only receive what he needs from One Being. I wholeheartedly agree with Gift Gugu Mona's words, "Only God can fill it." I also concur with Job's words that man's days are relatively few in relation to time and eternity, and those days are full of trouble.

Conception brings joy when a pregnancy is planned; joy also comes with some unwanted pregnancies. Before the child is born, there is a baby shower in which gifts are presented. He is the focal point of attention from the embryonic stage all the way through the gestation period. There is a mystery to every birth; neither parent knows what the child will turn out to be. They have hope and aspiration that he will be the next great man. Hope is nothing but a desire and an expectation. There is no guarantee that desire and expectation will manifest into reality—a man who will have a positive impact on the world—but they really don't know. Based on nurturing and the decisions he makes in relation to the void, he can be famous or infamous, good or evil. While newborn babes, could anyone tell that Adolf Hitler and his Nazi entourage would commit the atrocities they committed? The answer is, "No," in terms of specifics, but the void in man's heart and soul means the propensity and proclivity for evil lie dormant in him, awaiting opportunity. Crisis always presents opportunities for good or evil, for light or darkness.

I don't know for a fact, but I can take an educated guess that mothers and fathers of men who have gone onto infamy hoped and expected the best for them when they were conceived and birthed. I don't believe in speaking in absolutes when it comes to most things, but I believe it is safe to say most parents want the best for their children. A desire to see their children succeed motivates parents to make many sacrifices to achieve that goal. If it was just a matter of a loving, hard-working parent, family members, or guardians, most children would do great. Unfortunately, there are other factors which shape the heart and mind—factors which will determine what kind of human being the man-child will become. Some factors are internal while others are external. One of the factors is the nature the man-child inherits. Another is the external world he enters once he exits his momma's matrix. The intricacies and nuances of his thought pattern and personality may not be known right away, but any and everyone who is alive knows the kind of world into which he enters.Once he enters the world, there is a struggle which takes place within. An excellent treatise is given on this by Apostle Paul in his letter to the Romans. *"For I know that in me (that is in my flesh), dwelleth no good thing: for to will is present with me; but how to perform that which is good I find not"* (Rom. 8:18). "Flesh" is a reference to the nature in every man who is conceived and birthed. The struggle takes place between the desire he has to do what is right based on the teachings and instructions he receives, and the dark nature within which pulls him towards evil.

Once in the world, he will attempt to manipulate Momma or any other caretaker to get what he wants. I say his momma because she is the primary nurturer created via the womb which incubated him, the placenta which nourished him, and the mammary glands which provided life-sustaining milk to feed him and strengthen his bones. At a very early age he learns he is the center of attention; as a cute baby he learns early on to milk the attention and affection given to him to get what he wants. Here is the problem, left unchecked, his infantile desire to have things his way will morph into a manhood that is chaotic for himself and the sphere in which he has an influence.

Contrary to what some may think, believe, and say, it is not in the nature of an unregenerate man to consistently do what is good and moral. Given certain circumstances, he will choose darkness over light. This behavior begins in infancy. He has to be told not to put his hand in the cookie jar, and not to lie about taking the cookie once he has eaten it, while the crumbs are on his face. Where does he learn to do things he is told not to do, then to lie to cover his tracks? No one has to teach him; it is in his nature to do it. At some point in his adult life the cookie jar may become a bank he decides to rob, a home he invades to steal the homeowner's possessions, or the money he decides to embezzle from a business. It may be the child he molests, the woman he decides to rape, or the corner, house, or building from which he sells drugs. The list is long, and I could have gone on and on. Some of the examples are extreme, but real.

A man may read this and say, "Hold up, wait a minute. I have never raped a woman or molested a child." That is great, BUT like me, you battle with thoughts which are ungodly and you have skeletons in your closet—deeds done in the dark you hope and pray never come to the light. All of us have them in varying degrees, and if a man says otherwise, he is deceived or is a liar. If you doubt or are in disbelief, I invite you to take an honest look at your thoughts and actions; take a look back into history, both past and recent. Allow history to be the arbiter and judge. Pick a continent, any continent in the world, and I will tell you what has happened.

Genocide, Slavery, Colonization, Rape, Plunder, and Pillaging. What is sad about all of this is, on some occasions, these things have been done in the name of religion. Here are some examples: the genocide perpetrated against the indigenous people who occupied the lands known as the Americas before European settlers arrived; the Aztecs of Central Mexico; the Incas in Peru; and the Arawaks, also called Tainos, who were the original inhabitants of Jamaica, the island on which I was born. An online article in *The Harvard Crimson* dated October 12, 1996, has this to say about celebrating Columbus Day: "*When Columbus arrived on Cuba, Hispaniola, and other islands in the Caribbean he instituted shockingly cruel and genocidal policies which rapidly decimated the populations of indigenous Arawak Indians. He was also a slave trader.*" African people snatched from their homelands were crammed into slave ships like sardines and sold as chattel to work on the plantations of slave owners—whipped, and/or lynched when they attempted to break free from the shackles of physical, mental, and

4

emotional slavery. White audiences, who included men, women, and children attended lynchings during the Jim Crow era as if they were going to a fair or an outing. Between 1945-1946, approximately six million Jews plus others were killed by the Nazis. The list of atrocities is long and speaks to the depravity of the human heart, mind, and soul—a depravity which manifests through every man who is void of God consciousness. Mankind has produced great accomplishments in this world. There is no denying that, but the evil intentions of his heart have been displayed across the world. As terrible as all that sounds, all is not lost, because there is a way his vile, corrupted nature can be fixed. To know what that way is we have to go back to what I call...

THE POINT OF ORIGIN

From whence does the darkness which fills the void in a man's soul emanate? Human lineage can be traced through DNA, the human genome. Once traced, his DNA will take you back to the first man and woman to inhabit the earth. Once you get to his original progenitors, you learn why he had the void which darkness occupies, and why it causes a propensity and a proclivity for him and all men to manifest the fruits of a soul inhabited by darkness. The darkness which fills the void will cause a struggle within as long as he lives. Try as he might, he finds himself thinking and doing things which take a toll on his mind over time. I honestly do not believe there is a man alive who can honestly say he does not struggle with thoughts and actions which are considered evil.

CAUSE AND EFFECT

Every effect has to have a cause; reactions are the result of an initiating action. So, there has to be an explanation for everything in this world. I wholeheartedly agree with the reason for man's condition as recorded in the Bible—disobedience to and rebellion against his Creator. My argument for the existence of this Creator is based on my previous verbiage referencing cause and effect, action and reaction. Once the disconnect occurred between The Creator and His created beings, a vacuum was left; as previously stated, where there is a vacuum, invariably something is going to occupy the space, either light or darkness. Unfortunately for mankind, the something is evil. The only solution—the only hope for man—is to be reconnected to his Creator, to be born again of His Spirit, and to be recreated in His Image and Likeness. Void of this Light, man will habitually succumb to dark and evil thoughts and actions.

CHAPTER 2

THE STRUGGLE WITHIN

Waste no more time arguing what a good man should be. Be one.
—Marcus Aurelius

Throughout the history of the United States Marine Corps, many recruiting slogans have been used. One of the most memorable ones to me is, "The Marines are looking for a few good men." I would imagine the idea being the Marines would train a few good men to be great fighting men. They didn't want any kind of man—if they did, the slogan would not target the few, but would focus on quantity and not quality. Another one of their slogans is, "The Few. The Proud. The Marines."Who or what exactly is a good man? And how does the Word of God refer to a man's goodness? As an adjective, an online dictionary defines the word "good" as, "*to be desired or approved of. Having the qualities required for a particular role.*" As a noun, "good" is defined as, "*that which is morally right; righteousness.*" It is not farfetched to think that a man who is moral would be a man God would desire to use. Unfortunately, a man's morality does not gain him points with God. God's standard for goodness is God Himself; therefore, no man could be considered good in the eyes of God.

A man may feel that he is good based on the things he does and does not do, but the only goodness that is acceptable to God is that which comes from the righteousness imputed to man by God, through the Lord Jesus Christ. If we are willing to be honest as men, we will readily admit that all of us have thoughts, desires, and actions we don't want exposed. Since we know those thoughts, desires, and actions would shock people, we know they are not acceptable to God. So, what do we do? We mask them and hope no one ever discovers them. We camouflage and cover them up by doing public moral deeds. In the play, *As You Like It*, by William Shakespeare, the character Jacques speaks these words:

"All the world's a stage / And all the men and women merely players / They have their exits and their entrances / And one man in his time plays many parts."

The Marines need a few good men. Shakespeare said men are players who play many parts. God is not looking for good men, and He certainly is not looking for men who are players—He is looking for men who are willing to surrender to His Will, His Purpose, His Plans. He is looking for men through whom He can radiate and manifest His Light. The standard for goodness where God is concerned is extremely high, and scripture reveals this. Luke 18:18 records a certain ruler who called Jesus good and asked Him what he could do to inherit eternal life. Jesus' first response to him was, *"Why callest thou me good?"* Jesus' response seems peculiar since we know from reading and studying the scriptures that He was and is the goodness of God personified.

My personal belief is Jesus was very careful and meticulous in making sure people were directed to His Father in Heaven. He knew that at some point He would be received up into glory to the Right Hand of Majesty, and he wanted to make sure that man's standard of goodness was based on Him who sits high and looks low. He went on to tell the ruler emphatically, *"None is good, save one, this is, God."* If God Almighty is the only One who is inherently good, then there is no man who has the kind of goodness that is acceptable to God. A man's goodness is synonymous with his own righteousness, and the Bible does not use euphemisms, nor does it use enticing words to describe man's righteousness. God spoke succinctly through His prophet Isaiah: *"But we are all as an unclean thing, and all our righteousnesses are as filthy rags; and we all do fade as a leaf; and our iniquities, like the wind, have taken us away"* (Isa. 64:6).

When a serial killer or a rapist is caught, family, friends, and neighbors of the individual are usually shocked because this individual was someone they thought was a good person based on their public persona veneer and their good deeds. Some would go as far as to describe the man as a model citizen. These men were adept at compartmentalizing—hiding the side of them society considers abhorrent. When a person is bound by certain desires and appetites he knows society frowns on, he will go to great lengths not to be exposed, especially when those actions are criminalized. In order to ease his conscience to give the public a certain perception, he will overcompensate by putting effort into works and deeds—hoping family, friends, and people in his community will hold him in high esteem. If left unchecked, and if he does not receive deliverance, at some point in that man's life the ungodly desires, the insatiable appetite for perversion, etc. will cause him to act upon those desires, leading to exposure, which will cause him to be ostracized, shunned, imprisoned, or even killed.

In chapter 7 of Apostle Paul's letter to the church at Rome, he addresses the struggle within not only men, but all mankind. In the Life Application Bible there are three headings in Romans 7: "No Longer Bound to the Law," "God's Law Reveals Sin," and "The Struggle Within." The Holy Spirit's words through Paul will challenge every man who is honest to take an introspective look at himself, to see areas in his life that are in bondage and under the dominion of sin. A man who is honest with himself is willing to recognize and deal with root causes which compel him to commit acts like verbally abusing his wife and children. Where there is fruit there must be a root.

Men who desire to walk in the fullness and the fruitfulness of their Creator know they have to do constant fruit checks. These checks are needed to determine what type of fruit is being produced in a man's life. Is it the fruit of righteousness or is it the fruit of unrighteousness? Unfortunately, some men have become so debauched and reprobate in their minds, they actually enjoy the pleasures of sin (that only last for a season) because their consciences have become seared. For the man who is remorseful and repentant, the words written by Apostle Paul in Romans 7:24-25 should offer hope, and comfort. God—through Jesus Christ—can and will deliver the man who is willing to recognize his wretchedness and come to a place of repentance. Men, God Almighty is calling you! *Come now, and let us reason together, saith the Lord: though your sins be as scarlet, they shall be as white as snow; though they be red like crimson, they shall be as wool*" (Isa. 1:18).

If you as a man recognize yourself in the actions listed above, and you have suffered silently because of negative thoughts and deeds—thoughts and actions that have destroyed your marriage, destroyed your relationship with your family, caused you to be locked up, or ostracized—take this opportunity to confess and repent to God Almighty. He is merciful and forgiving. Cry out to Him and He will hear and He will answer you. He is one prayer, one confession, one repentance, one cry away. He desires to deliver you. Repent and call upon the name of the Lord Jesus Christ, Yeshua ha-Mashiach, and God will save, deliver, and set you free. No longer do you have to be a slave to sin; with true repentance, you can and will be a child of God—a man of God.

Some of the examples of the wretchedness of man listed above are extreme and most men do not fall into those categories but innate in all men is a proclivity for ungodliness. The man who becomes born again cannot and should not expect carnal thoughts and desires to disappear at the waving of some divine magic wand. He has to feed his inner man a constant diet of God's Word. He has to maintain a posture of vigilance where fasting and prayer are concerned. He must spend time in worship with his Creator God. He must deny his flesh by closing his ear and eye gates to things that stimulate the carnal nature. In a nutshell, he must heed Apostle Paul's instruction to, "Die daily."

CHAPTER 3

THE LIGHT

Darkness cannot drive out darkness; only light can do that.
—*Martin Luther King Jr.*

THE SOLUTION

Light's truest purpose is to do what the honorable Dr. Martin Luther King Jr. wrote, "Light is the only thing that can drive out darkness." When you enter a room that is dark, the first thing you do is turn on the light. Without the light, you would grope around in the dark, risking bodily injury. Once you are able to turn the light on you feel safe; you feel a sense of relief because you are able to see, able to navigate the space with ease. Job 12:25 says this about people in the dark: "*They grope in the dark without light, and he maketh them stagger like a drunken man.*" Darkness causes people to grope and to stagger because it is extremely difficult to maintain balance when there is no light. For this reason, God Almighty wants His Light to be on in our rooms—our bodies.

Light is something you may take for granted. For most of us, when we enter a dark room there is a switch not far from our fingertips. For obvious reasons, the switch is usually near the entrance. That switch allows us to turn on the light, which dispels the darkness. If only we had such a switch to turn light on in the dark areas of our minds. As far back as all of us can remember, at a certain point in the new day we see the light of the sun. In the nighttime we see the stars and the moonlight that is reflected from the sun. I've often wondered how people who are born blind or become blind deal with the inability to see light. Human beings are resilient creatures who have the ability to adapt to their environments. Knowing the importance light has in our everyday lives causes me to have great respect for anyone who has to navigate daily living without the ability to see.

John Lennon was a singer-songwriter and member of the legendary group, The Beatles. One of the many songs he wrote was called, "Imagine." He wrote it in early 1971, less than a year after the split of The Beatles. In the first stanza he wrote,

> *Imagine there's no heaven*
> *It's easy if you try*
> *No hell below us*
> *Above us, only sky*
> *Imagine all the people*
> *Livin' for today.*

With all due respect to the deceased Mr. Lennon for his prowess in singing and songwriting, I am going to refer and defer to the words written in Genesis 1:1 which states, "*In the beginning God created heaven and the earth.*" I will also refer and defer to the fact that there are fifty-four verses in the Bible where hell is mentioned. The thing about the imagination is that it is the forming of a mental picture of something not present, especially of something a person has not known or experienced. Imagination is not based in reality; whereas, the words in the Bible have transformed lives from the time men began to read and apply it. It continues to do so, and my belief is it will continue to do so as long as it is necessary—proving its authenticity and veracity. I don't have to imagine what the condition of the world would be without the existence of Heaven and hell, synonymous with good and evil, respectively. With the belief that many across the world hold of the existence of both Heaven and hell, we continue to live in a world of increased darkness and evil. Prophet Isaiah articulated it in his writings, *"For, behold the darkness shall cover the earth, and gross darkness the people"* (Isa. 60:2). The gross darkness described there will come from mankind—from people who think and feel they can do better living independently from God.

To give an analogy between light and dark, I will utilize the word Mr. Lennon used in the first line of his song, *"imagine."* It's an interesting choice of words in light of the manner in which Genesis 6:5 describes man's thoughts and imagination: *"And GOD saw that the wickedness of man was great in the earth, and that every imagination of the thoughts of his heart was only evil continually."*

With those words in mind—imagine for a moment a world without light. Imagine for a moment that nothing was bright. What would happen if the sun did not rise? Would you wake up and be surprised? I would emphatically say, "Yes!" How chaotic the world would be if darkness is all you could see. Imagine the impact on the roads, especially when you consider some folks' reckless driving habits. Since traffic lights have been invented, you don't have to imagine; picture in your mind how driving would be if there were no traffic lights.

What would happen if we relied solely on the judgment of the people driving? The answer is obvious, there would be a great deal of carnage. The traffic light lets us know when to stop, when to go. Red for stop, green for go, amber for slow. When people ignore the light, wrecks, death, and destruction are the results. As in the natural, so in the spiritual. When spiritual light is ignored, darkness will gain a foothold. The ensuing result will be the same: death and destruction. There is a reason why many crimes are committed when it's dark. It's obvious—the criminal does not want to be seen committing the crime because he or she feels they have a greater opportunity of not getting caught if no one sees them.

This world, this universe, created by The Most High has a certain balance to it. I believe it is based on the balance denoted by the saying, "you reap what you sow." Some people put it this way, "karma is real." I would encourage everyone to consider the words spoken by Yahshua written in Luke 12:3, *"Therefore whatsoever ye have spoken in darkness shall be heard in the light."* Since words spoken in darkness shall be heard in the light, then it is safe to say deeds done in darkness will be revealed by the light, meaning ultimately no one gets away with any deed done in the dark. No matter how long it takes, dark deeds must come to the light for judgment.

LET THERE BE LIGHT

When I am reading, writing, or studying a particular subject in the Bible, I look to see where it is first mentioned. In writing this chapter on light, I followed that methodology and went to Genesis, the book which records beginnings and first mentions. I saw something concerning light that blessed and amazed me. This is what I saw. The first recorded time we see and read words spoken by The Most High is in Genesis 1:3, which reads, *"And God said, 'Let there be light.'"* When God speaks something, it must manifest. When He called light into being, darkness had to give way. When He saw the light, He saw that it was good. Since light represents goodness, it is safe to say darkness represents evil. Please distinguish between the darkness night brings, which allows us to rest and serves other purposes for the earth as eloquently referenced in the foreword by Mr. Laval Belle, and the kind of darkness the Bible references, which comes from the wicked one, the facilitator of evil.In writing about men being void of light, yet created by the Father in Heaven to be witnesses of the Light, I feel it necessary to mention the different forms of light referenced in the Holy Bible. The first book of Genesis reveals to us how The Most High dispensed with the darkness that was upon the face of the deep; it also shines light (no pun intended) on the different kinds of light He called into existence through His omnipotent power and authority. Verse 16 tells us He made two great lights: the greater to rule the day and the lesser to rule the night. This reference is to the sun which gives light for the day, and the moon which reflects the light of the sun in order to give light by night. Stars were also created to help humans navigate through earth. Years later, wise men would travel seeking Him who was born king of the Jews. When they found Him they said, *"We saw His star in the East."* According to verse 18, light rules; light separates. Since The Most High called light good, men void of light are in bondage to darkness—to that which is not good, and therefore is evil. They are slaves to evil in its varying degrees. No matter how they try to appease their consciences with good deeds or with religious activity, their hearts remain deceitful, desperately wicked, and in need of Divine Light.

The Divine Light I refer to is not the light needed by the earth, by mankind, to see clearly or for photosynthesis. As previously stated, The Most High gave humanity the sun, the moon, and the stars for those purposes. I am referring to a different kind of light. It is the Light of the glorious goodness of our Father in Heaven—revealed in the fullness of His Godhead bodily through the *Logos* incarnate, manifested in bodily form. John said He was in the beginning with God, and He was God. John wrote, *"All things were made by Him; and without Him was not anything made that was made"* (Jn. 1:3). As I was speaking with my friend Laval Belle about various types of lights, he said something profound: as brilliant as the sun is, it pales in comparison to the Divine Light.

God Almighty dwells in blazing light. His very being is the fullness of light. His glory is radiant. Even the sun that floods our planet with light has dark spots. There are no spots on God—no hint of a blemish. As the Apostle James declares, *"Every good gift and every perfect gift is from above, and comes down from the Father of lights, with whom there is no variation or shadow of turning"* (Jas. 1:17).[1]

As brilliant as the sun is in its radiance—in the plethora of ways it helps the universe—its brilliance pales in comparison to the effulgent radiance, to the glorious splendor, of The Most High God—Creator of the universe.

LIKE FATHER, LIKE SON

Through shared DNA, sons have a likeness to their fathers, not only in physicality, but also in speech and other mannerisms. Since God Almighty is Spirit, His sons should have and manifest His spiritual attributes. Thoughts can translate into action and the manifestation of the spiritual can be seen in the natural. The Most High is described by James as the Father of Lights, so all His sons should endeavor to exude, exhibit, and exemplify His attributes of Light. In the same manner in which the Father of Lights has neither spot, wrinkle, nor blemish, He made provision for all His sons to be full of light. He did it by sending His only begotten Son, the Holy One, who came in His Image and in His Likeness. We know this because His Word tells us via a conversation He had with a disciple named Philip, *"Philip saith unto him, Lord, shew us the Father, and it sufficeth us. Jesus saith unto him, Have*

I been so long time with you, and yet has thou not know me, Philip? He that hath seen me hath seen the Father and how sayest thou then, Show us the Father?" (Jn. 14:8-9).

Sons of God—men of God in whom the Light of God dwells—should be able to say the same thing to those who inquire about Father God. They should say, "When you see me, you see my Father." A man can't say that if he is not manifesting Godly Light. Yeshua let us know God is not every man's Father. This is what He told some Pharisees: *"Ye are of your father the devil, and the lusts of your father ye will do. He was a murderer from the beginning, and abode not in the truth, because there is no truth in him. When he speaketh a lie, he speaketh of his own: for he is a liar, and the father of it"* (Jn. 8:44-45). Men of Light must not be murderers and liars; they must shine their lights to help others live their best lives—they must speak truth. Live long enough and you will hear the saying, "Action speaks louder than words." If you consider yourself a child, a son of God, then you can't just talk about it, you must be about it; not just in words but in deeds.

THE WORD OF LIGHT

> *The entrance of thy words giveth light;*
> *it giveth understanding unto the simple.*
>
> —*Psalm 119:130*

Have you ever heard someone described as or called a simpleton? A simpleton is a foolish or gullible person. Psalm 19:7 states, *"The law of the LORD is perfect, converting the soul: the testimony of the LORD is sure, making wise the simple."* With this scripture in mind, we can say a simple person is one who lacks wisdom. In the Life Application Bible, the author of Psalm 119 is listed as anonymous, though it also says some suggest Ezra the priest is the author. When the Almighty's Word enters a place, when it is applied by someone, it dispels the darkness of ignorance. It gives light—which in this case is akin to wisdom, knowledge, and understanding—to the gullible, foolish man. Transforming him from a simple man to a wise man, it also shows how dark a man's heart is without light, in other words, without the Word of Light.

In the same manner in which the Holy Bible differentiates light, it also differentiates darkness. In one sense darkness is the absence of light; in another sense, darkness correlates with evil and with wickedness. In chapter 3 of the gospel written by John, Yeshua taught a pharisee named Nicodemus the importance of being born again of the Spirit; failure to do so would leave mankind open to condemnation. We are not left in ignorance concerning this condemnation. Yeshua said,

"And this is the condemnation, that light has come into the world, and men loved darkness rather than light, because their deeds were evil" (Jn. 3:19).

There are three key points of utmost importance to take note of in the words of Yeshua recorded in John 3:19:

1. He was referring to Himself when He said, *"Light has come into the world."*
2. The reference is to sin-laden men who loved darkness more than they loved Him.
3. He does not leave us ignorant as to the reason why they loved darkness—it is because they loved doing evil deeds.

FOOLS

The legendary reggae singer Dennis Brown (RIP Dennis Emmanuel Brown), who Bob Marley called, "The Prince of Reggae," wrote a song called, "Why Fools," in which he asked the question, "Why fools don't know themselves?"

In his song, "Only a Fool," Luciano sang,

"Only a fool / Says in his heart / that there is no God /
But in his heart / He must be mad /
Who made the sun to shine? /
And who rules the end of time?"

When I put the lyrics of both exceptional singers together, they reveal to me that the foolish man is the man who does not acknowledge the existence of The Creator God who made the sun to shine—the Omnipotent, Omnipresent, and Omniscient One who Luciano said rules the end of time. A man who denies the existence of His Creator is in darkness and can never know himself until he acknowledges His Creator and manifests His will—in thought, word, and deed. The reason being is what I stated earlier. Man was made in the image and likeness of The Creator to manifest light, but yielding to sin caused and yet causes him to operate in the image and likeness of the deceiver, the liar, the murderer.

Every word spoken by The Most High is priceless. The fact that His first words called light into being is evidence of its importance. When He said, *"Let,"* He uttered a divine imperative, a command. On page eight of his book, *The Holiness of God,* published by Tyndale House Publishers, Inc., Dr. R.C. Sproul wrote, "God called the universe into being." The theologian and church father Augustine called that act "the divine fiat." A "fiat" is an imperative or a command. Further, Apostle Paul's second letter to the Corinthian church confirms the aspect of creation concerning light. The apostle wrote: "

For God, who commanded the light to shine out of darkness, hath shined in our hearts, to give the light of the knowledge of the glory of God in the face of Jesus Christ"(2 Cor. 4:6).

The condition of the earth described in Genesis chapter 1 necessitated the commanding of light to shine. The earth was without form, and it was void; darkness was upon the face of the deep. The Holy Spirit's words through Paul in 2 Corinthians 4:6 are analogous to the words spoken by God Almighty as recorded in Genesis 1:3. The God who said, *"Let there be light: and there was light,"* has shined His glorious Light in our hearts. Our reference is to men and women who recognize and realize the void within, and the need to fill the void with light. The Holy Spirit told us through Apostle Paul why The Most High shined Light in the heart of man, *"To give the light of the knowledge of the glory of God in the face of Jesus Christ.* Here we see the correlation and connection between light and knowledge. We also see where Light is found—*"In the face of Jesus Christ."*

Without the knowledge of Christ-Mashiach, the heart of man has no light. The ensuing result— dark thoughts and deeds continually reflected in depraved actions. Don't get me wrong; a man will at times do acts of good because of conscience, teachings, and instructions imparted to him. With that said, he will invariably give heed at some point to the dictates of a sin darkened soul if he has not received the Light of the World to rule and reign on the throne of his heart. Be not deceived but discern God's True Light as opposed to the pseudo light manifested through vessels used by the deceiver. The Lord gives explicit warning against this deception via His words written by Apostle Paul in 2 Corinthians 11:14, *"And no marvel; for Satan himself is transformed into an angel of light. Therefore, it is no great thing if his ministers also be transformed as the ministers of righteousness; whose end shall be according to their works."*

It's not too difficult to discern whose minister a man is—just look at his works. Are they the works of light, or the works of darkness? Are they the works of the Spirit, or the works of the flesh? Men, don't straddle the fence; don't attempt to play both sides from the middle. There is too much at stake in terms of how you will be rewarded for eternity. How you fare in the end will be determined by the works you manifest in the time allotted to you in the earthly realm. My advice to you and to myself is use your God-given time wisely. His gift of time to you is a precious and valuable commodity, so don't waste it in folly. One day you will have to give an account. BE FOREWARNED!

CHAPTER 4

THE HEART OF
THE MATTER

The heart is deceitful above all things,
and desperately wicked: who can know it?
—Jeremiah 17:9

W hen addressing the heart of any matter—you are dealing with core issues. The core issue with any man is this: who is ruling on the throne of his heart? Is it The Almighty One or is it the wicked one? Are his actions reflective of a mind and thoughts which are full of light? Is he radiating Divine Light or is he manifesting demonic darkness? Please hear my heart, men. Let us not deceive ourselves or allow the enemy to deceive us. No man will be able to plead ignorance. No man will be able to say, "I didn't know." The Bible is clear and detailed in listing the works of the flesh which come from an unregenerate heart—a heart void of light.

Now the works of the flesh are manifest, which are these;
Adultery, fornication, uncleanness, lasciviousness, idolatry,

*witchcraft, hatred, variance, emulations, wrath, strife, sedi-
tions, heresies, envyings, murders, drunkenness, revellings, and
such like: of the which I tell you before, as I have also told you
in time past, that they which do such things shall not inherit
the kingdom of God.*

—Galatians 5:19-21

People are taken out of wills and lose their inheritance because
they fall out of favor with the person who wrote the will. Look at
the Bible as God's will through Christ who died to give mankind
an inheritance of eternal life. A man cannot live his life according
to the dictates of the carnal mind—manifesting the works of the
flesh and expecting not to fall out of favor with The Almighty
One. Falling out of favor is tantamount or akin to losing his inheritance of eternal life and not having his name in the Book of Life.
Temporal euphoric pleasures of sin for a moment are not worth
an eternity in darkness, void of light—absent from the presence
of the Father.

Every man must take an honest assessment of his life; no man
should look at himself through rose colored lenses. There are no
euphemisms used in describing the wretchedness of the human
heart when it is dominated by the sin nature. The Word of God
is both clear and concise in the manner in which it describes the
unregenerate heart. That heart is capable of conceiving the most
wicked thoughts which a man will act upon at every opportunity. Prophet Jeremiah used the words, "deceitful" and "desperately wicked" to describe it. Concerning the heart, The Most High
asked His people through the mouth of His prophet, "*Who can
know it?*" My answer to that question is God knows it. He knows
it better than us because He is omniscient.

I am going to go as far as to say we do not know the fullness
of deceitfulness, nor do we know the fullness of how desperately

wicked our hearts are; that is, until a situation arises which breeds the manifestation. Apostle Paul used the word "our" in referencing the heart because no one has an exemption from needing Divine Light. The reason being is that all human hearts, minds, and souls are darkened with deceitful, desperate, wicked, and ungodly thoughts and desires.

A man who looks at himself through rose colored glasses, who is unwilling to recognize the true state of his condition, is a man who is seriously deceived—a man who will not be delivered until he recognizes his condition and repents. He will continually return to deceit, to wickedness, like a hungry dog returning to its vomit. The intent here is not to gross you out; it is to bring awareness and recognition that each man must look in the mirror. He must yield his thoughts, attitudes, and his actions to God if he hopes to be free from the darkness which filled the void created by the disconnect from his Creator. Without this freedom, his eternal home will not be the Kingdom of Light. Honest self-assessment will lead every man to ask the important question—what is the condition of my heart? Is it deceitful, is it desperately wicked? Is it steeped in darkness or is it radiating Divine Light? I have a favorite Shakespearean quote that I quote often. It appears in his most famous play, *Hamlet*, and it gives us one of his most quoted lines:

"To thine own self be true." It's a nice quote—BUT! My belief is this: a man can only be true to himself and others if he is true to Almighty God. By denying that he has darkness in his heart, he denies the need to have the glorious Light of God to shine in and through it; he tells God he does not need to repent—he does not need to change. The problem with this type of thinking is the deceived man thinks he has the approval of his Creator. He operates in a pseudo light which comes from the wicked one who sits on the throne of his heart. The one who convinces him that he can lie, cheat, steal, and kill with impunity. He absolves himself of

the responsibility of seeking God for change by making excuses for his actions or making futile attempts at self-justification.

As my friend and brother in the Kingdom Mr. Reggae Paul Henry says, "There is no gray area here." There are no shades of gray. It is clear and it is to the point. Yeshua has ministers and Satan has ministers. The difference between them is like the difference between night and day, light and darkness. A man is not a servant minister of Yeshua because "Christian" is listed on his birth certificate in the section that asks for religion. He is not a servant minister because he grew up in a family that attended church consistently. He is a servant minister of Yeshua in right standing with God Almighty when he receives and allows the Divine Light to replace the darkness. Like a diamond that has come through the rough, he refracts and reflects The Almighty's goodness by being a bearer and witness of the Light.

In one of his hit songs, the silky, smooth singer Sam Cooke sang, *A Change Is Gonna Come*. If I had had the opportunity to speak with Mr. Cooke, I would have told him change does not come—it needs an initiator to bring it to pass. Without an initiator, the status quo will remain the same. When the issue is a deceitful, desperately wicked heart, a heart void of light, the initiator of change must be the man who recognizes the fruit of darkness manifesting in his actions; he must recognize his powerlessness to break ungodly habits. He must recognize his need for the Father of Lights. He must recognize his need for the One James called, *"The Father of lights with whom is no variableness, neither shadow of turning"* (Jas. 1:17).

Man must humble himself and cry out, "Father, where are You?!" He can survive and overcome life in the earthly realm without his biological father, albeit with difficulty; there is no hope of an eternal life of peace without his Spiritual Father. Psalm 27 was written by David, and its theme is God offers help for today and hope for the future. Unwavering confidence in God is our antidote for fear and loneliness. In verse 1 David wrote: *"The LORD is my light and my salvation; whom shall I fear? The LORD is the strength of my life; of whom shall I be afraid?"* The words of the first verse of this Psalm lets us know that where there is no salvation, there is no light. Without the LORD, there is no light, no salvation—only the lack of strength, fear, and many other negative things too numerous to name because of time and space constraints.

CHAPTER 5

MAN BORN OF WOMAN

Trouble is the common denominator of living.
It is the great equalizer.
—Søren Kierkegaard

There is a passage of scripture found in the book of Job which paints a picture of mankind after the fall of Adam. The words in the scripture provoke me to examine myself whenever I read it. The words are, *"Man that is born of a woman is of few days, and full of trouble"* (Job 14:1). When The Most High presented the woman to Adam, he called her bone of his bone and flesh of his flesh; He called her Eve (*Chava*) which means, "life giver." Genesis 2:18 states, *"And the LORD said, it is not good that the man should be alone; I will make him an help meet."* She was taken from him and given to him to be his *ezer neged* (helpmeet), which means, "a front, a counterpart, other side, one who is suitable for him." Both Adam and Eve were made in The Creator's Image and Likeness to manifest His Light in the earth. He blessed them and instructed them to be fruitful and multiply. Their offspring would be fruitful, they would multiply, they would reflect Divine Light.

Both male and female made a choice which caused a disruption to the flow of the garden paradise The Most High gave them for their dwelling place. I will go into more detail about that disruption later. One of the consequences of the disruption is recorded in Genesis 3:16, "*Unto the woman he said, I will greatly multiply thy sorrow and thy conception; in sorrow thou shalt bring forth children.*" Every male, every female, is birthed through pain and sorrow. If you are unaware of this, please ask any woman who has given birth about third trimester contractions. Speak to a mother who has experienced postpartum depression and you will get an idea of what is written in Genesis 3:16. David, the sweet Psalmist of Israel writes, "*Behold, I was shapen in iniquity; and in sin did my mother conceive me*" (Psa. 51:5).

With that in mind I understand why Job described a man born of a woman as of a few days, and those few days as full of trouble. A man can live to the ripe old age of one hundred plus, but his life is relatively short when you think about eternity. If a man lives to the ripe old age of one hundred and twenty, which is the age listed in Genesis 6:3, and you subtract the years when he had to be taken care of by parents or guardians, then subtract the years when age takes its toll on his mind and body—negatively impacting his quality of life—the years he is able to live a reasonable quality of life are relatively short in the larger scheme of things. So, Job is right when he spoke about man having a few days. A short life and it full of trouble is not a good combination. Man either makes trouble or he has trouble inflicted upon him by a troublemaker. Whatever fills a man's heart, mind, and soul is what he will manifest. A man who is full of trouble will spread that trouble wherever he goes. Try as he may, trouble will plague him for the duration of his life, because it is innate. Job went on to say: "*He cometh forth like a flower, and is cut down: he fleeth also as a shadow, and continueth not*" (Job 14:2). Like a flower that comes out of the ground in the spring and brings joy to lovers of nature, the newborn brings joy until he starts to give trouble, which causes sorrow.

I once heard someone say, "Wisdom comes with age." On the other hand, I heard someone else say, "There is no fool like an old fool." A man who lives to a certain age should gain and apply wisdom from the lessons life has taught him—especially the difficult lessons. It is one thing to behave foolishly when you are young and lack experience; however, once a man reaches adulthood, you would think he would have put away foolish behavior. Unfortunately, that is not always the case. There are some men who have aged chronologically, yet their decision-making process does not reflect wisdom, knowledge, and understanding. It is like the inmate who is a recidivist; every time he is released, he goes right back to a life of crime which returns him back to prison.

Almighty God expects the man who submits his will to Him to operate in a spirit of wisdom which flows from a knowledge of His Word. Through the spirit of adoption, he becomes a new creature, or should I say, a renewed creature. Although correct, Job's statement probably was influenced by the great tragedy which had befallen him. Full of trouble does not only refer to what is in man's carnal nature, it also refers to the trouble he will encounter by virtue of being alive, by virtue of being in a world dominated by darkness.

Many years ago, I heard someone say, "Trouble doesn't last always." Although trouble doesn't always last, it seems as if it lasts longer than the moments in life when a man has joy and happiness. The majority of a man's life is one form of trouble giving way to another. Trouble can be likened to a storm; a man's life appears to consist of a series of storms—he is either coming out or going into one. Some storms last longer than others; some storms are more destructive than others. At certain points in a man's life, he may have to deal with multiple storms simultaneously. He may have only a short time to recover between each storm. It is not a matter of **if**, but **when** a man will be hit with storms of varying categories. According to the Bible, "*The sun shines on the just and the unjust.*" King Solomon wrote:

> *I returned, and saw under the sun, that the race is not to the swift, nor the battle to the strong, neither yet bread to the wise, nor yet riches to men of understanding, nor yet favour to men of skill; but time and chance happeneth to them all.*
>
> *—Ecclesiastes 9:11*

All men, whether swift or slow, whether strong or weak, whether wise or foolish, whether rich or poor, will all endure troublesome storms as long as they live. The difference is men who are full of Yah's Spirit may encounter trouble, but they are no longer full of trouble. They don't go looking for trouble, but when trouble finds them, they have the wisdom to know how to deal with it.

They have renewed minds which give them the ability to discern how they should navigate and operate through the trouble. Like a muscle, a mind must be exercised or it will suffer atrophy.

There are individuals in society who are very health conscious. They are disciplined in their eating habits and exercise regularly. They are lean and muscular from a regimen of weightlifting and cardiovascular exercises. "*For bodily exercise is profitable to the body, albeit a little according to the Bible: For bodily exercise profiteth little: but godliness is profitable unto all things, having promise of the life that now is, and of that which is to come*" (1 Tim. 4:8). A ripped, muscular body is great for the earthly realm; it can give a great deal of confidence to the person who trains. In the Kingdom realm, glorified bodies will be needed; renewed minds will be needed. The man whose mind's focus is the Kingdom is not worried about the troubles and struggles he experiences in life. God Almighty has set eternity in his heart and that is where his focus is. He lives his life on earth in preparation for his life in eternity. He views all troubles and struggles in relation to what he will gain in eternity with the Father. He is a Romans 8:18 man, *"For I reckon that the sufferings of this present time are not worthy to be compared with the glory which shall be revealed in us."* These are men who know that troubles, struggles, and present time sufferings represent times and seasons of preparation for promotion in their lives.

Let me speak poignantly to my brothers and sisters behind prison walls, as well as to others behind mental walls of depression and despair.

Brothers and sisters, those of you who live in an environment with troubles and struggles on every side, God Almighty wants to use your experience to reveal glory in and through you. Please do not allow your environment and the madness you have to deal with trap your minds in depression and despair. Keep your eyes on the prize—an eternity with the Father of Lights in Glory.

I am not asking you to do something The Most High has not challenge me to do. When I was locked down with madness all around, with grown men acting like clowns, what did I do? I doubled down in the Word, in prayer, and in praise. The ensuing result was that I saw glory manifest in and through me; I saw the glorious Light of the gospel shine in a dark place. I saw that glorious Light impact cold-hearted, hardened men. The Word will never lose its power—it is the antidote for any and all troubles and struggles. All you need to do is live it. Bodily exercise is necessary, but not to the exclusion and neglect of mental exercise.

A grave problem occurs when there is no balance in terms of quality time spent exercising the mind in the principles of the Kingdom of God, principles that can only be gained by study and meditating in God's Holy Word. As great as a chiseled, toned physique can look, at some point that body will succumb to the ravages of the aging process. Good eating habits and exercise may help a person live longer; it may help him to maintain soundness in mind, body, and soul over a longer period of time. But cosmetic surgery notwithstanding, all human bodies will return to the dust from whence man came. Troubles and struggles in life can and will shorten a man's life if not dealt with properly. The stress of it can cause the young to look aged.

The balanced man is the man who works diligently in order to have a mind, body, spirit, and soul which operate in unison and are suitable as a temple for the Spirit of God. A balanced man refuses to allow his life to be heavy-laden with troubles and struggles to the point of being ineffective. I repeat, he is a man who understands the importance of balance. When I used to go to the prison gym to work out, many of the men worked hard on their chests, biceps, shoulders, triceps, and all the other muscles in the upper body. Only the faithful few worked hard on their legs, because working the quadriceps and calf muscles was extremely painful. I know I was one of the ones who spent a lot of time working my upper body to the exclusion of the lower, until one day, someone told me if I kept doing it like that, I would wind up looking like Mr. T. Not the TV character Mr. T, but Mr. T in the sense of having broad, muscular shoulders with skinny legs.Some men are spiritual Mr. T's. They look strong and well put together on the outside but have little to no inner spiritual strength. They are not strong in prayer and fasting and lack strength in praise and worship. They are anemic and emaciated in their study and meditation of God's Holy Word. This causes them to be incapacitated when trouble comes. The lack of balance means they are easy prey for the adversary. Men who don't pray will become prey. Like Adam their progenitor, they will not be able to guard, protect, or stop the serpent from entering and negatively transforming their environment. However, Yeshua was able to repel the adversary's attack in the wilderness with the words,

"It is written." The best defense they will be able to muster is the Adamic one, the anemic one, the excuse one: "The woman you gave me, she is the source of my problems." In order to avoid taking a realistic introspective look to find and deal with the root of the trouble, they prefer to point the finger at others: "I was abused as a child, abandoned by my girlfriend/my wife." "I was raped/molested which left me busted, disgusted, barely able to be trusted." These are legitimate issues men have to deal with, but they should be used as steppingstones not stumbling blocks.

Like any other man, God's man has a set time to be born and a set time to die according to Ecclesiastes 3:1. In between birth and death he will experience troubles, some beginning when he is in the womb. The difference is God's man works on himself from the inside out, not from the outside in. He is not superficial in his desire to look good on the outside; his desire flows from his inner spiritual connection to his Creator—a connection which gives balance and equilibrium to his mind, body, and soul. His inner man is permeated by the fruit of God's Spirit. While other men are full of trouble, he is full of the Spirit with all the fruit and blessings the Spirit provides.

So, man that is born of a woman is of few days and full of trouble—BUT—man born of the Spirit is for eternity and will be full of Glory.

WHEN THE STORM BREAKS

When I was in the final stages of writing the manuscript for my book, *Great Women,* my wife and I saw a movie that had great dialogue about a storm titled, *Elizabeth—The Golden Age.* It portrayed the life of one of England's great monarchs. The film depicted a time when Spain was the most powerful empire on earth and her King, Philip, was a staunch Catholic who plunged the world into a holy war.

Only England stood against him with her Protestant Queen. Half of the English population were Catholics at the time, so he attempted to foment dissension against her from within her own country, while he prepared his ships to attack. As the Spanish Armada of ships were sailing towards the coast of England and the nation was preparing for war, Queen Elizabeth met with her spiritual advisor hoping he could give her some glimmer of hope of victory against the advancing enemy. At one point in tears, she asked him, "Give me hope." He replied, "The forces that shape our world are greater than all of us, Majesty. How can I promise they will inspire in your favor even though you are the queen?" Then he spoke the following words which awakened something in her, words which bless me tremendously every time I read them, words I believe will inspire every man who is dealing with troubles, struggles, and difficult storms.

He told the queen, "But this much I know, when the storm breaks, each man acts in accordance with his own nature. Some are dumb with terror. Some flee. Some hide. And some spread their wings like eagles and soar on the wind." His words caused her countenance to change. As she arose from a somber and pensive posture, I saw the nature of the eagle rise up in her. She told him he was a very wise man, to which he responded, "You are a very great lady."

MEN

When the storm breaks in your life, what nature will you act in accordance with, the Divine or the defeated, the lion or the beagle, the chicken or the eagle? When the storm breaks, will you be dumb with terror, will you flee, will you hide, or will you spread your wings like an eagle and fly? When the storm breaks, men sent from God rise to the occasion. They spread their wings and prepare to soar. They open their mouths and prepare to ROAR!

CHAPTER 6

MAN OF GOD OR WOMAN'S MAN

A woman wants a man she can look up to—
one who will not look down on her.

—Anonymous

There should never be room in the heart of a Man of God for covetousness. Give no place, give no space to that kind of evil; it violates God's ninth commandment. When David coveted Uriah's wife Bathsheba and sent Uriah to be killed, not only was the ninth commandment violated, but the fifth, which states, "*Thou shalt not kill.*" That was not the last time there would be a violation of both the ninth and fifth commandments. It is seen again in an equally egregious scheme involving a husband and wife team, a king and queen—Ahab and Jezebel. Theirs was the most toxic relationship in all of the Bible, a relationship wrought with evil—void of balance. A relationship in which the king was dominated by the queen, to the point where he became feckless and reckless. There are some men who should never enter into the covenant of marriage until their vile, corrupt hearts are transformed. By themselves they can do a great deal of damage; when they team up with another person of low moral turpitude, the union breeds a combustible combination.

There is a particular spirit I've heard about on many occasions since I've been in church. It is called the "Jezebel spirit." Once I started reading her story, I asked myself a question, "Where was Ahab?" The term "Jezebel spirit" is used to malign some women unfairly. It is also used to define some women's behavior fairly. Jezebel could not have gotten in the door without a weak enabler like Ahab. You want to stop a Jezebel? Find the Ahab who enables, facilitates, and capitulates to her schemes. As wretched as her acts are, she does not act alone. She operates with a weak co-conspirator. A scripture to prove my assertion that the operation of a Jezebel spirit manifests when someone gives her the room she desires is Revelation 2:20-23, in which Yeshua speaks to the angel of the church of Thyatira:

> *Notwithstanding I have a few things against thee, because thou sufferest that woman Jezebel, which calleth herself a prophetess, to teach and to seduce my servants to commit fornication, and to eat things sacrificed unto idols. And I gave her space to repent of her fornication; and she repented not. Behold, I will cast her into a bed, and them that commit adultery with her into great tribulation, except they repent of their deeds. And I will kill her children with death; and all the churches shall know that I am he which searcheth the reins and hearts: and I will give unto every one of you according to your works.*

There was a hit song when I was growing up that had these lyrics, "God don't like ugly / He's gonna make you pay for what you done to me." There are times when He makes the children of the wicked pay. The Jezebel of Thyatira was given room to operate by the angel-leader of that church. Her namesake who was married to the weak, covetous Ahab, was just as cold blooded if not more so. There are some men who get their leadership position by appointment, while others get theirs through inheritance. Ahab inherited the throne of Israel from his father Omri who established a dynasty. Ahab married Jezebel, the daughter of Ethbaal, king of Sidon in hopes of expanding the dynasty. Men, be careful who you say, "I do," to! The problem for him was that he was no match for her cunning, calculating ways. His weakness opened the door for her to convince him to abandon Yahweh in order to introduce the abominable worship of Baal to Israel. There is a story in 1 Kings 21 that highlights how lethal and treacherous their combination was. It is the evidence to show that men with Ahab-like tendencies should never marry a woman like Jezebel—especially when they are in leadership.

A man by the name of Naboth had a vineyard near Ahab's palace. The vineyard had been in Naboth's family for a long time; they probably had a thriving wine producing business. Covetous Ahab decided he wanted Naboth's vineyard to grow a vegetable garden. He expected Naboth to give it to him in exchange for another vineyard he felt was better. Land or other property that has been in a family for generations is special and the owners will not part with it even when offered large sums of money; Naboth was no different. *"And Naboth said to Ahab, The Lord forbid it me, that I should give the inheritance of my father's unto thee"* (1 Kgs. 21:3).

Naboth's response should have been sufficient enough to curb Ahab's greedy, ungodly lust for his vineyard. Naboth told the king the Lord forbade him from giving it away because it was the inheritance of his fathers, meaning it would be handed to his children and his children's children. Certainly, Naboth and Ahab would have known Yahweh's instructions to Israel that, *"A good man leaves an inheritance to his children's children."* Land was very significant to the Israelites because it was included in the covenant blessings promised to Abraham by Yahweh.

Wickedness in the heart of a man, if left unchecked, can reach a place where they lose their fear of God.

Ahab went home in a fit of rage like a spoiled child who did not get what he wanted. A spoiled, enraged child can get a time out or a spanking; what do you do with a grown man who acts like a tantrum throwing child? Or a man who is married to a wicked, scheming ungodly woman? You watch God deal with them. Ahab went home, got in his bed, turned away his face, and refused to eat. He paints a picture of a pathetic, weak man—a man who is a king and a leader of God's people acting like a juvenile delinquent.

A weak, immature man who acts like a juvenile is like a puppet on a string to a conniving, cunning woman he is in cahoots with. Weak men always attract strong, domineering women with "Jezebelic" tendencies. A strong, Godly woman will not settle for a weak man with "Ahabic" tendencies. If for some strange reason she hooks up with one, the relationship will not last.

Jezebel came to her husband and asked him why he was sad—why he was not eating. Like a momma's boy or a child speaking to his domineering, controlling mother, he told her he asked Naboth for his vineyard, *"And he did not give it to me."* It sounds like a scene from a kindergarten class or schoolyard when one child wants another's toy and throws a tantrum when he is refused. A fair minded, conscientious wife would have told him to get out of bed, end the pity party, eat some food, and forget about the man's vineyard—unfortunately, Jezebel lacked those qualities. Her response was to challenge his leadership ability by asking him the question,

"Dost thou now govern the kingdom of Israel?"

That was a loaded rhetorical question asked to stir him from his place of pathetic, infantile retreat. In other words, "You are the leader of the kingdom of Israel, so why are you acting like that?" Her idea of leadership was dictatorial—just take what you want and to hell with the consequences. Her next words to him live in infamy and set in motion a chain of events which led to bloodshed. She told Ahab:

"Arise, and eat bread, and let thine heart be merry: I will give thee the vineyard of Naboth the Jezreelite" (1 Kgs. 21:7). Instead of being the *ezer neged* (helpmeet) in the God sense of the word, she decided to help him by stealing another man's property; she acted as an instigator. Her words could have easily been, "Cheer up. Mommy is going to get it for you." He didn't care how she got it, as long as it came into his possession. A Man of God's desire for something should not be so overwhelming he is willing to obtain it through malfeasance.

When a government needs to acquire private lands for a project it deems beneficial for the greater good, the government can apply the Law of Eminent Domain. It is the right of a government or its agent to expropriate private property for public use, with payment or compensation. There was no such Law of Eminent Domain in King Ahab's desire to possess Naboth's vineyard—God forbade Naboth from giving or selling the land, and Ahab wanted it for his personal use. If Naboth would not give it or sell it to him, then Ahab would get it through nefarious means.

The woman he married had no qualms about killing to get what she wanted. They are the Bonnie and Clyde of the Bible—a toxic, lethal combination of abuse of power.

In order to steal Naboth's land, Ahab allowed her to commit a heinous, ungodly act using the King's seal. She wrote, signed, sealed, and delivered a letter as if it came from Ahab. Men, be careful of who has access to your important documents. She sent the letter to the elders and nobles of the city and she conspired with two false accusers, described in the Bible as men of Belial. The name Belial means, "without profit, worthless, destruction, wicked, evil, and ungodly." These men testified that they heard Naboth blaspheme against God and the king—his fate was sealed. They stoned him and Jezebel told Ahab to take possession of the vineyard.

God's leading man must be a man of the highest ethics, character, and integrity. His leadership style must come from a heart that loves and fears God. Ahab does not appear to be as wicked as some of Israel's kings who preceded him. Aside from his covetousness, his problem was he was a weak man; his weakness was exacerbated by the person he chose for a wife—a woman who personified evil and wickedness. God's man needs a companion who will not be an enabler of his ungodly desires—a companion who will motivate, inspire, and encourage him to do righteous acts. Maybe without a wife like Jezebel, Ahab would have desired but not acted upon his desire to covet and take Naboth's inheritance. The combination of his weak leadership with Jezebel's "get it at any cost" mentality wreaked havoc upon the nation of Israel during their time as king and queen. God's man must be meticulous in his selection of the queen he chooses to reign with him. If he chooses a Jezebel, she will exploit his weaknesses through manipulation and witchcraft.

The prophet Nathan was sent by God to expose David's covetous and murderous acts (more on that later); likewise, God sent His prophet Elijah to expose and pronounce judgment upon Ahab and Jezebel for what they did to Naboth. God does not violate his principle of coming to the man, the head of the family, when there is a crisis. Although Jezebel appears to be the one in the marriage who wore the proverbial pants, and she was the one who instigated and initiated the attack on Naboth for his vineyard, Elijah was sent to Ahab first to expose, then to pronounce divine retribution. God spoke to Adam first, then He addressed Eve. A Man of God must not relinquish his responsibility of leadership. He must not allow himself to be enticed, seduced, or manipulated into committing ungodly acts; if he does, judgment will be pronounced prophetically.

Ahab and Jezebel's punishment was severe, but God will not punish anyone and not show mercy if there is true repentance. His mercy does not mean His man servant will always escape some form of punishment. Like David before him, Ahab repented and received mercy from God. When Elijah told him what the punishment would be—he rent his clothes, put sackcloth upon his flesh, and fasted. The previous time that Ahab abstained from food was when Naboth refused him his land. This abstinence came from a penitent heart, so it was a fast. God honors a fast that emanates from a repentant heart.

"And the word of the Lord came to Elijah the Tishbite, saying, Seest thou how Ahab humbleth himself before me? because he humbleth himself before me, I will not bring the evil in his days: but in his son's days will I bring the evil upon his house" (1 Kgs. 21:28-29).

No man is an island. What a man does has a collateral effect on the people connected to him—especially his wife and children. Someone may say, "His sons are innocent, why should his evil come upon them?" In the eyes of God, all have sinned and come short of His Glory. God is a God of the families of the earth. He is a generational God; He warned His people to teach their children His laws and statutes. God's order is violated when a man abdicates his responsibility as His leader; the consequences of the violation will be calamitous. A leadership vacuum leaves an opening for someone who does not have the heart of God to take charge.

CHAPTER 7

"YOU THE MAN"

If you want to see the true measure of a man,
watch how he treats his inferiors, not his equals.
—*J. K. Rowling*

When I was growing up in Corona Queens, New York, the brothers had a saying when another brother did something they considered awesome; one brother would say to another, "You the man." It was a form of recognition and affirmation that something cool had been done. That term has its origin in the Bible, but not in recognition or affirmation of something cool or awesome. On the contrary, it was spoken by a prophet named Nathan when God's King David committed the horrible trespass of sending one of his soldiers named Uriah to the front of a heated battle so he could be killed. Why would the king do something so atrocious? For the same reason many men commit murder—so they can have the man's wife or something else of value they covet.

Although David was called, *"a man after my own heart"* by God, the sweet psalmist of Israel was still a man, and like other men, carnal desires that are not dealt with will lead to dire actions and consequences. Second Samuel describes a time when kings go forth to war. David was a true soldier and warrior for Yahweh who led men on the battlefield. Instead of going on the battlefield, he sent Joab, his servants, and all the fighting men of Israel. They put in work by destroying the children of Ammon and besieging Rabbah.

David tarried still at Jerusalem (2 Samuel 1:1). Jerusalem is a great place to tarry, but not at a time when you should be leading God's army on the battlefield. Tarrying is good when you are doing it in the presence of the LORD, awaiting instructions. However, when you tarry at a time you are supposed to be taking care of a serious matter, it can and will become problematic. On many occasions I've heard the saying, "an idle mind is the devil's playground."

When evening came, David got out of bed and walked up to the roof of the palace. While on the roof, he saw a very beautiful woman washing herself. Kings have a certain amount of sovereignty; however, their power and authority must be balanced with wisdom and prudence. The Bible warns us about the lust of the eyes. Women are beautiful and they are to be viewed and admired, but not in a lustful manner.

Blessed is the man that endureth temptation: for when he is tried, he shall receive the crown of life, which the Lord hath promised to them that love him. Let no man say when he is tempted, I am tempted of God: for God cannot be tempted with evil, neither tempteth he any man: But every man is tempted, when he is drawn away of his own lust, and enticed. Then when lust hath conceived, it bringeth forth sin: and sin, when it is finished, bringeth forth death.

—James 1:12-15

The crown of life is not received when a man fails; it is received when he endures and overcomes temptation. He is able to overcome temptation because of his love for the Lord and the indwelling of God's Word and the Holy Spirit, both of which empower him to be strong in the Lord and in the power of His might. When a man does not spend time reading and meditating in God's Word, choosing instead to feed his carnal nature, he will not be able to endure and overcome temptation. Whatever he lusts after will entice him and cause him to be drawn away; he will be lured away from the presence of His Creator who dwells in light into a place of darkness. If he chooses to stay in that dark place, sin will eventually consume and destroy him. Based on what the Holy Spirit wrote through James, God Almighty is not to be blamed. It is the lust within that gives the wicked one an opening to entice and lure him away. This is why it is important for every man to fill his heart with The Almighty's Word. David said, "*Thy word is a lamp unto my feet, and light unto my path*" (Ps. 119:105). A man void of The Most High's Word is a man traveling a dark path. David also wrote, "*Thy word have I hid in mine heart, that I might not sin against thee*" (Ps. 119:11). The Word gives light, and it is a buffer against sin.

Like many other men—myself included—David ignored the warning from God's Word when he inquired of the woman. He was told her name was Bathsheba and she was the daughter of E-li-am—most importantly—she was the wife of Uriah the Hittite. Naming her father let David know where she came from. Naming her husband let him know she was another man's wife. The latter should have stopped him in his tracks, but lust can consume a man's mind, causing him to make decisions he will regret.

His inquiry should have ended there. In that time and dispensation, kings had harems which allowed them to choose which woman they wanted to be with at any given time. Bathsheba was off limits, not only because she was married to another man, but her husband was a brave, valiant soldier who fought for David. David sent messengers to get her and when she came to him, he slept with her. Afterwards he heard the words men who have slept with someone else's wife dread to hear—especially men who have their own wives and children—I'M PREGNANT! The cover up is usually more problematic than the sin; desperation breeds irrational thoughts and actions. In order to cover his misdeeds, David called Uriah from the battlefield and told him to go to his house and wash his feet. David also gave him a large portion of meat. Uriah didn't go home; he chose to sleep at the door of the king's house with all the other servants of King David. When David asked him why he had not gone home, Uriah replied:

"The ark, and Israel, and Judah, abide in tents; and my lord Joab, and the servants of my lord, are encamped in the open fields; shall I then go into mine house, to eat and drink, and to lie with my wife? As thou livest, and as thy soul liveth, I will not do this thing" (2 Sam. 11:11).What an honorable man he was. By choosing to stay at the king's door, he unwittingly and unknowingly signed his own death warrant. David made one last desperate attempt to get him to go home, hoping he would sleep with his wife. He fed Uriah and made him drunk, but Uriah would not go home. Men, be careful who you are eating and drinking with; he may be a Judas. In a desperate, deplorable, and despicable attempt to cover his misconduct, David wrote a letter and sent it to Joab. In the letter he instructed Joab to set Uriah in the forefront of the battle, then to pull the troops back from him so he could be killed. The saddest part of the sordid affair was he had Uriah deliver the letter.

Man is not what he thinks he is, he is what he hides.

—André Malraux

The heart is deceitful above all things, and desperately wicked: who can know it?

—Jeremiah 17:9

All men have hidden things, things they desire to remain secret. The best thing for a man to do is to repent and turn to His Creator so he can receive His love and forgiveness. Divine Love does not condemn, it covers. According to 1 Peter 4:8, *"Love shall cover the multitude of sins."* Divine Love, known as *agape* love, is deep enough and wide enough to cover the most heinous and egregious transgressions. Men, do not allow yourself to be tormented by a past transgression; just repent and The Most High will cast it into the sea of forgetfulness. After repenting, allow Him to fill your heart with His love while you fill your heart with His Word. These are key things which will enable and empower you to resist any and all temptation. It is not a matter of **if**, but **when** temptation will come. When it does, you must have The Most High's instruments in you as a bulwark—a defense against sin's encroachment.

We can hide our transgressions from others but not from The Creator. He has all-seeing eyes. He sent His Prophet Nathan to have a conversation with David who was living large and in charge in the palace, albeit with a woman whom he had received through malfeasance and nefarious means. His enemies were subdued all around, and he was truly living like a king. Whenever we think we are in a place of peace and safety and we have hidden sins, sudden destruction will come. It is only a matter of time. Men, get out of the dark and come into the Light of the Father.

RESTORE THE LAMB

When Prophet Nathan came to David, he didn't come pointing his finger and wildly accusing the king of murder; he was very strategic and told David a story:

And the Lord sent Nathan unto David. And he came unto him, and said unto him, There were two men in one city; the one rich, and the other poor. But the poor man had nothing, save one little ewe lamb, which he had bought and nourished up: and it grew up together with him, and with his children; it did eat of his own meat, and drank of his own cup, and lay in his bosom, and was unto him as a daughter. And there came a traveler unto the rich man, and he spared to take of his own flock and of his own herd, to dress for the wayfaring man that was come unto him; but took the poor man's lamb, and dressed it for the man that was come to him.

—2 Samuel 12:1-4

David did not realize he was the rich man described by Nathan. In the palace he had a harem of concubines from whom he could choose to lie in his bosom. Like most, if not all of us, David was furious when Nathan told him the story. We want the guillotine for someone who has committed an appalling act, but mercy when we are caught doing something atrocious. His anger was greatly kindled against the man, but the proverbial shoe never fits nor does it feel good when it is on the other foot. David said:

"As the Lord liveth, the man that hath done this thing shall surely die: And he shall restore the lamb fourfold, because he did this thing, and because he had no pity" (2 Sam.12:5-6).

And Nathan said to David, **"YOU ARE THE MAN."**

Honestly, how many of us as men have been that kind of man? Maybe not to the extent of sending someone to be killed or killing someone to take control of his wife or some other valuable possession. It may not have been a wife or a girlfriend, but money, jewelry, drugs, or something else that is valuable. It is important to note again, the desire in David to commit such an egregious act is in all men to a greater or lesser degree. He truly loved God, just like you do—BUT! Your sanctification—my sanctification—is an ongoing process when we are in God. In Corona, Queens, the city that I referenced at the beginning of this chapter, I knew people who were killed so that their drug block and their drug spots could be taken over. During the crack epidemic of the 1990s, that was the norm in cities all across America. And how many people have killed or hired someone to kill a spouse so they could collect the insurance?

Nathan reminded David of all the Lord had delivered him from and delivered to him. God told David that He gave him his master Saul's house and his wives. God gave him the house of Israel and Judah. And if that was too little, He would have given him much more.

Greed and covetousness are terrible sins that will take you farther than you want to go, keep you longer than you want to stay, and cost you more than you want to pay. Are the ends justified by the means? Absolutely not! If a man could see the ensuing results of devastation and destruction his action would cause, most men would abandon their course of destructive action. Men are behind the prison wall right now because they refused to heed warning signs. I know because I was one of them. On many occasions during my sentence, I pondered how things would have been different if I had heeded the warnings. As bad as it was, it worked in my favor because it was behind the wall where I came across John 5:39-40 and read the words, *"Search the scriptures; for in them ye think ye have eternal life: and they are they which testify of me. And ye will not come to me, that ye might have life."* The life I had lived up to that point was void of light—filled with darkness. There was no relationship with the Heavenly Father. On March 6, 1991, all that changed when I surrendered and Father God delivered me from the darkness and brought me into His marvelous Light. Men, He is no respecter of persons. He can and will do the same for you!

God called what David did, *"Despising the commandment of the Lord and doing evil in His sight."* Because of the transgression, evil would be raised up against David's house, and that which he did to Uriah in taking his wife, would happen to him and much more. The sinfulness of man will never escape the omniscient gaze of Almighty God. Any attempt to hide sin is an exercise in futility. I remember a time I was invited to speak at a conference and the theme was, "Watch God." When I stood up to minister, I told the people my subject, "God is Watching." He is called the Ancient of Days, but His eyes have not dimmed with the passing of time. He is watching; He still passes judgment on sin. His final words through Nathan to David as far as that sordid affair was concerned was,

"For thou didst it secretly: but I will do this thing before all Israel, and before the sun."

The use of the words, *"before the sun,"* is interesting when you think of the fact that the light of the sun is extremely bright. The idea being, David's sin against The Most High in taking Bathsheba and sending her husband Uriah to be killed would be exposed for all to know. Over two thousand years later, people all over the world are reading about it. Let this be a warning to all of us; the pleasure of sin for a season, whether long or short, is never worth the punishment the transgressors will receive. Repentance gives us a pardon for the day of judgment, but there are ramifications which have to be dealt with in this realm. David's household would be decimated. His son Amnon would rape his sister Tamar, and his beloved son Absalom would kill his brother Amnon as revenge for the rape of Tamar. Absalom would lead an insurrection against David, driving him from the palace into temporary exile, and Absalom would sleep with his father's concubines:

Then said Absalom to Ahithophel, Give counsel among you what we shall do. And Ahithophel said unto Absalom, Go in unto thy father's concubines, which he hath left to keep the house; and all Israel shall hear that thou art abhorred of thy father: then shall the hands of all that are with thee be strong. So they spread Absalom a tent upon the top of the house; and Absalom went in unto his father's concubines in the sight of all Israel.

—2 Samuel 16:20-22

How ironic. Absalom slept with his father's concubines on the roof; David was on the roof when he saw the very beautiful Bathsheba washing herself and decided to sleep with her. Here is another irony found in 2 Samuel 23:34, Ahitophel is listed as the father of Eliam who was the father of Bathsheba. The suggestion of some scholars is that he was Bathsheba's grandfather. Some people describe payback as a (blank). I will allow you to fill in the blank.

I've never met a man who wanted his sordid sins—the skeletons in his closet—to be exposed. Many men have committed suicide when their hidden transgressions were leaked to the public. The prospect of living with the shame, the stigma, and the ridicule being much more than they could take, they chose death as their way out. As bad as David's actions were, he was truly a man after the heart of God—which meant taking responsibility and his repentance. *"And David said unto Nathan, I have sinned against the LORD. And Nathan said unto David, The LORD also hath put away thy sin; thou shalt not die"* (2 Sam. 12:13).

Once an action is undertaken it cannot be undone. Thankfully, remorse can be felt, atonement can be made, and repentance can be offered in hopes there will be forgiveness. The story reveals that God forgave David and spared his life because he was truly remorseful and repentant; however, there had to be stringent punishment meted out because of the importance of his position. As king and leader over God's people, he set a dangerous tone. Men, by the grace of Almighty God, we must endeavor to live lives that are beyond reproach. None of us are perfect, but some things must not be associated with us. In the event that we fall, we must not make matters worse by attempting a cover-up; we must confess our sins before God Almighty. We also must be willing to make restitution if it is possible.

CHAPTER 8

WHAT MANNER OF
MAN ARE YOU?

*Nearly all men can stand adversity, but if you
want to test a man's character, give him power.*

—*Abraham Lincoln*

THE STORM BEFORE THE CALM

This chapter's title echoes the question asked by Jesus' disciples who were on a ship caught in a great tempest. Their question was in response to Jesus' rebuke of the boisterous winds and the sea which had caused them great fear. At Jesus' command, there was a great calm.

They had never seen, nor had they encountered a man who had such command over the elements of nature. They could not comprehend how He was able to exert such power and authority. I am sure being Jews, they had heard and read of all the miraculous things Jehovah had done through Moses and the prophets, but in the ship with them was One who was greater than them all.

They should have understood, based on their reading and studying of Bereshit/Genesis, when Jehovah created man, He gave him dominion in the earth, which gave man the ability to subdue it. By the time Yeshua manifested in the earth, man had long relinquished the authority and dominion given to Him by his Creator. The disciples in the ship were so overwhelmed with fear of the ship sinking and taking them with it, they probably could not think straight. As previously stated, fear fosters irrational thoughts and actions. Prior to calming the storm, Jesus asked them why they were fearful. After asking them the question, He gave them the answer—it was because they were so fearful and bound, they could not exercise faith.

Pressure will reveal the manner of man you are. How a man responds to a pressurized situation reveals his level of maturity and preparedness. At some point in life, every man will face a situation that will test his mettle. The New Oxford American Dictionary defines the word "mettle" as: "*a person's ability to cope well with difficulties or to face a demanding situation in a spirited and resilient way.*" Men who are full of Divine Light—bearers and witnesses of that Light—have spirited resilience gained from overcoming various challenges through the power of God's indwelling Spirit. Through the power of the Spirit, he builds and develops habits which prepare him not only to survive, but to overcome storms of varying degrees and categories. He is not frustrated, nor does he become discombobulated when his life is hit by a virulent storm. When he encounters a dark situation, he allows Divine Light to radiate, with the ensuing result being the transformation of the atmosphere.

The man who is void of Divine Light, who is not a bearer and witness of the Light is the opposite. He cannot offer a spirited, resilient response to a dark, pressurized situation because he is not yielded to the Father of Lights. His tendency is to fight fire with fire—darkness with darkness—which only exacerbates the situation. He has to rely on other things like his intellect and his wits to survive. Unfortunately, no matter how sharp that man's mind is, how much wealth, education, power, and authority he is able to wield, there is a level of darkness he will face that will plunge his heart and his mind into fear—a level that his human intellect, his power, and his prestige cannot negate. The man who chooses to fill the void in his life with the Father's Divine Light is able to navigate through the darkest times of a crisis, coming out better and greater than before. He is able to do so because his focus is fixed on Christ in the crisis—the Christ who is the Light of the World. The One in whom the fullness of the Godhead dwells bodily according to Colossians 2:9. Men who are full of Light do not lose their moral compass by attempting to use carnal means and methodology to alleviate a crisis. The Most High has tested, tried, and purified them in the furnace of affliction. That man is able to face any and all obstacles because God does not promote anyone before He has tested them for the level they will occupy.

I can use myself as an example here. When I was in English lockups and prisons like Wormwood Scrubs, Brixton, Belmarsh, and Swaleside, I could have chosen to indulge in the prison underworld. Instead, I chose not to allow more darkness fill my soul, which would correlate with darker actions—an extremely challenging undertaking as anyone one behind the wall will tell you. It is an extremely challenging task because of the psychological and physical warfare which is a constant part of prison life. Meekness can be taken for weakness in a hostile environment where you are surrounded by people who are trying to get over, trying to catch you slacking and lacking. I put my trust in The Most High for peace and protection by immersing myself in The WOL (Word of Light). I was in a dark place, and it was a dark time and season of my life, but I purposed in my heart, mind, and soul no more would I be a man void of Light. No more would I roam the corridors of darkness in thought, word, and deed. No more would I live a life void of a relationship with The Creator. I cried out, "Father, where are You?" When I cried, by Grace and through Faith, He manifested in the dark cell and transformed my life. From that point forward I decided to dedicate my life to helping others fill the void in their lives which darkness had occupied. I knew the impact the Divine Light had on my life, and I wanted others to have that experience. I did back then what I continue to do today: I gave them my testimony of deliverance from darkness by the Father of Lights.

The man chosen to be the bearer and witness of the Light has a mission and a responsibility to help other men overcome the struggles with dark thoughts and deeds they face. He has to exemplify how someone overcomes tragedy through the power of the Spirit, as opposed to succumbing to a spirit of fear, which most certainly will plunge the individual into greater darkness. The greater darkness I refer to is that which is caused when the man under pressure uses pornographic perversion, drugs—legal and illegal—and alcohol in a futile attempt to self-medicate against the ravages of the storm. When that individual comes out of his perverted drug and alcohol induced stupor, he soon realizes that he has compounded the problem. He still faces the original problem, but now he also has the problem of a brain which craves more perversion, more drugs, and more alcohol in order to feel normal. Instead of rolling up a blunt, snorting some coke, chasing the dragon with heroin, shooting heroin, smoking crack or meth, or getting drunk, God's Light bearer and witness will pray, fast, worship, and meditate in the Word. His response is spiritual, it is not carnal. His resilience stems from a life that is rooted in a deep, committed relationship with Father God. He is not living a life in which God is an afterthought or the One to be called when there is a crisis, but forgotten about once the storm lifts.

He is the manner of man who prioritizes his relationship with his Heavenly Father. He seeks the Kingdom first with its righteousness. This priority gives him the comfort and confidence to know that God will add the things he needs no matter the severity of the trouble he faces. He is not cocky; he is confident. He is humble, yet bold because God's righteousness makes him bold as a lion. In the same manner that the lamp has to be plugged into a socket so electricity can cause the bulb to give light, God's man— His Light bearer and witness—understands he must maintain his connection to Yeshua, the Light of the World. He is cognizant of the fact that a lack of or severing of that connection will cause darkness to overtake him. He endeavors to keep his life plugged into the source of Divine Light.

There are plenty of examples around us of men who are Light bearers and witnesses for The Almighty, and men who are darkness bearers and witnesses for the wicked one. There is no middle ground as it pertains to light and darkness, when used to be indicators of good and evil. A man is either a bearer and witness of the Light, or he is a bearer and witness of darkness. Only what is inside him can come out of him, no matter how he tries to hide and mask his inner darkness, sooner or later, a situation will arise which will reveal the manner of man he is—a situation which will demonstrate whether he is full of Light or void of Light. It is evident in the things he says and the things he does. A man can perpetrate and pretend that he is an agent of Divine Light, but when he is tested, who he truly is will be exposed and revealed. If Divine Light dwells within, it will manifest; if darkness dwells within, it will manifest.

It is said, you can fool some of the people some of the time, but not all of the people all the time. God Almighty cannot be fooled at any time because He is all-knowing. Through His Word, He has given mankind all the information needed to understand what it means to walk in the light and what the consequences are of walking in darkness. The Bible is clear and succinct in revealing this to us because the penalty for living in darkness is very great. This is what Yeshua said:

> *And this is the condemnation, that light has come into the world, and men loved darkness rather than light, because their deeds were evil. For every one that doeth evil hateth the light, neither cometh to the light, lest his deeds should be reproved. But he that doeth truth cometh to the light, that his deeds may be made manifest, that they are wrought in God.*
>
> *—John 3:19-21*

If dark deeds were not sensually pleasing, and if condemnation was swift and without mercy, most men would avoid the darkness at all costs. God is merciful, He is long suffering, and He is patient. Men who do not have the Light of the Savior in them love the darkness because they think they will not be condemned. Unbeknownst to them, they are already condemned because of their refusal to repent and become receptacles of Divine Light. If they die in that state of darkness and condemnation, the wrath of God is what they will face.

There is no repentance once death causes a man to transition from this life. It behooves every man to check himself before he wrecks himself. He has to examine his deeds honestly and be man enough to make the necessary changes if they are dark. Some dark deeds are so ingrained in the hearts and minds of men, they have become the norm and not an aberration. Those men run the risk of having a reprobate mind—minds and habitual deeds which have become so darkened, there is no hope of them coming to the Light. Their consciences are completely seared by years—if not a lifetime—of lascivious and licentious living. Jesus described them as, "*Lovers of darkness whose deeds are evil.*"

When a person loves someone or something, they willingly give the lion's share of their time, energy, and finances to that person or thing. The man who has a sin darkened soul—the man who is led by the flesh and not by the Spirit—will by hook or by crook lie, cheat, and steal to maintain control. His manner is demonic and does not reflect the Deity of his Creator God. The demonic man reflects darkness in his thoughts, speech, and in his actions. God's man, the bearer and witness of Divine Light, reflects the Light in his thoughts, speech, and in his actions, especially when he faces a dark situation. His mannerisms exude the fruit of the Spirit, whereas the mannerisms of the man of darkness exude the works of the flesh.

A man's mannerisms are determined by the nature he is born with and the way in which he was brought up. The good thing is The Almighty has the power to give him a new nature—a Divine Nature—if he is willing to repent, to turn. The manner of man Jesus was and is displays One who has God's Divine Nature. He is the epitome of Divine Light for there is no darkness in Him. Through the born-again experience, men who have a desire to be Light bearers and witnesses will be sent out by The Creator. Their natures have gone through a metamorphosis, one which caused the darkness which plagued them from birth to give way to the new nature—a nature which makes them a new species. *"Therefore, if any man be in Christ, he is a new creature: old things are passed away; behold, all things are become new"* (2 Cor. 5:17).

CHAPTER 9

GOD SOUGHT
FOR A MAN

Talent is God given; be humble.
Fame is man-given; be grateful.
Conceit is self-given; be careful.
—*John Wooden*

G OD is Almighty; He is Sovereign—He is not account-
able to nor does He have to answer to anyone. I was
listening to Christian radio and heard a really good definition of the word "sovereign" as it relates to God. Pastor Greg
Laurie was interviewing author and radio host, Joni Eareckson
Tada. She has been in a wheelchair for over fifty years due to a
diving accident. This is what someone told her about the sovereignty of God at a time when she struggled with the idea of living
as a quadriplegic: "

God permits what he hates to accomplish that which He loves."
She used Jesus dying on the cross for the sins of the world as an
example.

If God had to answer to anyone, He would cease to be sovereign, and the one He answered to would be the true sovereign. He declared, "*For every beast of the forest is mine, and the cattle upon a thousand hills. I know all the fowls of the mountains: and the wild beasts of the field are mine. If I were hungry, I would not tell thee: for the world is mine, and the fulness thereof*" (Ps. 50:10-12).

In the thirtieth-eight chapter of Job, The Almighty challenged Job with a series of "who hath" and "canst thou" questions, such as: "*Who hath divided a watercourse for the overflowing of waters, or a way for the lightning of thunder?*" (Job 38:25). "*Knowest thou the ordinances of heaven? canst thou set the dominion thereof in the earth?*" (Job 38:33). His series of questions were asked to provoke thought in Job, and to let him know beyond a shadow of a doubt that He alone is God Almighty and beside Him there is no other. Although He is sovereign and all powerful, He does not violate His laws and principles—He does His work in the earth through man, because that is the sphere where He gave male and female dominion.

He told His prophet Ezekiel, "*I sought for a man.*" God Almighty never does anything that does not have Divine purpose, so He created the heavens, the earth, and living creatures. Then he created a man He called Adam. After creating him, God put him in a garden He had created eastward in Eden. Adam's assignment was to dress and keep the garden.

Once Adam was in the beautiful, idyllic garden, God created a woman whom Adam called Eve. He gave Adam and Eve dominion over all living things that moved upon the earth. When dominion was lost or surrendered through disobedience to God's explicit instructions not to eat of the tree of the knowledge of good and evil, God had a plan. And in line with His consistency, that plan involved sending a man to restore order to the chaos that sin had caused in His creation. Man forfeited his responsibility, so God would use a man to restore the responsibility.

Adam was told that he could eat freely from all the trees in the garden except that one.

When someone is told that they should not do something, if they don't guard their heart, temptation will tell them that is exactly what they should do. Unfortunately, Adam and his helpmeet Eve succumbed to the temptation and did exactly what God told them not to do, causing a void, a gap, a breach between them and their Creator—a void that would affect every human being because all human beings would trace their lineage to the first couple. *"And the Lord God called unto Adam, and said unto him, 'Where art thou?'"* (Gen. 3:9). Adam was made first, so The Almighty addressed him first when He came calling. If and when there is a problem in the church or in the marriage, when God comes calling, He doesn't call the deacon, or the usher first; He doesn't call the wife or the children first. He calls the man first. Prior to the fall, Adam walked and talked with God in the cool of the day. He exuded and manifested the fruit of God's *Ruach*—His Spirit—which are:

love, joy, peace, long-suffering, gentleness, goodness, faith, meekness, temperance.

The man God would use to bring restoration to His creation could not be void of Light, could have no works of the flesh—that would disqualify him from the assignment. He had to be full of Light; he had to have the fruit of the Spirit permeating and saturating every fiber of His being. He would be the anti-venom, who could cure and heal all mankind of the serpent's bite. Where would God find such a man since He could not find him on earth? With God, all things are possible. There was a problem, a dilemma, but fortunately there is no problem nor dilemma that is unsolvable for God. The problem and dilemma was that there was no man on earth capable of being God's instrument for redemption, because all men were connected by blood to Adam, therefore all men shared his DNA, which meant all had a nature corrupted by sin. This passage of scripture in the book of Ezekiel encapsulates the dilemma: "*And I sought for a man among them, that should make up the hedge, and stand in the gap before me for the land, that I should not destroy it: but I found none*" (Ez. 22:30).

Sin is something God will never tolerate. His righteousness demands that sinners be judged, and once found guilty, they must be punished. Sinful man deserved to be judged by the righteousness—the justice—of God. He cannot be bribed like some human judges. There is no high priced attorney that the sinner—the criminal—can hire to get him off the case. His position of power and prestige cannot help him. His family and his societal connections are meaningless when the judge is God Almighty.

When the darkness of sin is in a man's life, it may be sweet to the taste, but it will be bitter and poisonous to the stomach. It is akin to him digging a pit that he will eventually fall into, a pit that he will not be able to get himself out of. Sin is so deep, mankind needed a Savior; he needed a deliverer. The great self-deception is when a man thinks he can handle sin. The hedge was so badly broken, the gap which separated mankind from The Creator was so wide, there was no man with enough light in him to stand in the gap as a mediator; there was no man powerful enough to make up the hedge.

In Ezekiel's time, the people had perverted themselves because of sin; mankind became void of light and wickedness increased to the point where The Almighty was ready to judge them. The only thing standing between fallen mankind and The Most High's judgment was His mercy. One of God's other prophets, Jeremiah, said this concerning God's mercy and judgment, *"It is of the Lord's mercies that we are not consumed, because his compassions fail not"* (Lam. 3:22). In Jeremiah's and Ezekiel's day—and in our day—wickedness had increased in the land so much that divine destruction was imminent. The hedge was broken, and there was no man qualified to stand in the gap for the land. Truly a sad indictment on mankind. When the serpent entered the garden and beguiled Eve, and Adam partook of the sin, the hedge was broken, the gap was created, and creation was plunged into darkness. *"He that diggeth a pit shall fall into it; and whoso breaketh an hedge, a serpent shall bite him"* (Ecc. 10:8).

Our English vernacular does not do justice to our interpretation of scripture at times, so we have to look at what was spoken and written in the original language. "Hedge," as it is used in Ecclesiastes 10:8, is the Hebrew word *gâdêr* (pronounced gaw-dare¢) and it means, "an enclosure: a fence, a wall." It comes from the root word, *gâdar,* which means, "to wall in or around: close up, fence up, enclose." Disobedience and rebellion to God's instructions caused the hedge to be broken; the ensuing result being the separation of man from God. Since The Most High is the Father of Lights, whomever or whatever is separated from Him will be void of Divine Light, which is synonymous with Divine Goodness.

Adam's rebellion caused the hedge to be broken, and when it was broken, the serpent bit him. The bite corrupted his nature, and it went from Divine to carnal. The serpent's bite caused the ground he walked on to be cursed, and it caused his thoughts and actions to become void of Light. The characteristics and attributes which passed from Adam to all mankind are described by Apostle Paul in Galatians 5:19-21 as the works of the flesh: *"Adultery, fornication, uncleanness, lasciviousness, Idolatry, witchcraft, hatred, variance, emulations, wrath, strife, seditions, heresies,*

Envyings, murders, drunkenness, revellings, and such like." Paul went on to write, *"Of the which I tell you before, as I have also told you in time past, that they which do such things shall not inherit the kingdom of God."* The works of the flesh are inherent in every unregenerate man. Adam attempted to hide; he attempted to cover his shame—his nakedness—with leaves from a fig tree, to no avail. All men have attempted to hide from the omnipresent gaze of The Creator; they have attempted to expiate their sins with all kinds of coverings, to no avail. They have used many things to fill the void caused by sin, but all have been useless. A man was needed to make up the hedge, to stand in the gap. "Gap" has a similar meaning to hedge. It is the Hebrew word, *perets*, and it means, "a break, a breach." It comes from the root word *parats* which means, "to scatter." Disobedience to and rebellion against the Word of God will cause things to fracture, they will cause brokenness, and a scattering.

As previously stated, if you were to examine the history of nations and societies all around the world, what would you see? You would see the effects of sin, the effects of the broken hedge, the gap, and the void which darkness filled. In the same manner that certain diseases or the predisposition to certain diseases are carried through the blood, the propensity to sin came through the bloodline of Adam. It not only infected and affected the garden, but all of God's creation. Man is not sinful because he is in the world; the world is filled with sin because dark-hearted, sinful people are the occupants. It is evident for all to see: racism, sexual perversion, pornography, sex trafficking, rape, murder, lying, cheating, stealing, and the list goes on and on. No one in their right mind would dare to assert that man left to his own devices would choose what is righteous and Godly.

History has proven from the beginning that he never does. Does he do good deeds at times? Of course, he does! But that is the exception and not the rule. The rule is an unregenerate man, a man void of Divine Light, a man who is not in covenant with Father God, will always choose salacious, "soulish" satisfaction, because his desire for sinful pleasure is insatiable. Outside of restoration to a right relationship with Father God, his lustful desires are never satisfied. He is willing to risk everything—including his freedom—to fulfill his desire. When The Almighty One is not the focal point of a man's desire, that man will never have peace. The peace I am referring to is the peace which passes all understanding, guarding the heart and the mind. The further a man moves from the presence of Almighty God, the deeper and wider the gap becomes, the more darkness will fill that void.

It is like the drug addict who has such an insatiable craving, he or she will do almost anything to get the next hit, the next fix. Like the sex addict who is unable to resist his voyeuristic desire to look at porn (adult or kiddie), he is overcome by his craving to curb crawl in hopes of finding the prostitute who can satisfy his fetish. But no matter who he finds, he or she can only offer a temporary respite from the pull emanating from the stronghold of his carnal nature. He can vow a thousand vows, he can get counseling, he can promise his wife that he will never do it again, but his flesh will always win. The flesh will always win because there is only One who can truly satisfy him, and that is His Creator.

Psalms 16 ends with the words, "*Thou wilt shew me the path of life: in thy presence is fulness of joy; at thy right hand there are pleasures for evermore.*"

This text could have read, "Thou wilt shew me the path of Light, because Life with God is Life in the Light." Fullness of joy means there is no room for anything that causes sorrow. When the void in a man's life is filled with the joy of the Lord, he will not be overcome by temptation when it seeks an opening to lure him into sin. The fullness of the joy of the Lord gives him strength as confirmed by Nehemiah 8:10, *"The joy of the Lord is your strength."*

The void in a man's heart that is filled with darkness—the thing which caused him to be separated from His Creator—will eventually destroy him. There is only one solution to this problem: a Savior, a Redeemer, a Restorer of the breach who can deliver man from an eternity in darkness. The Savior, the Redeemer, would have to be Light personified—there could not be one iota of darkness in Him. He would be the One to deliver mankind from sin, and in turn, use delivered men to reflect His Light. The men would not be the hedge makers or the gap standers. Their assignment is to be bearers of Light and witnesses of and for Him. Their redemption by the Redeemer, the Savior, the Deliverer, would constrain them and make them feel compelled to reach other men still trapped in the condition they were delivered from.

They would be willing to visit the prisoner, to go into the drug dens, to the dens of iniquity, and to the houses of ill repute to tell bound men about the Savior. They would go with fullness of joy, radiating Divine Light. They would go with this testimony: but for the grace of God, there go I. They would go with the understanding Ezekiel received from God when He told him the land would be destroyed if God did not find a man to make up the hedge and stand in the gap before Him for the land. The question is: ARE YOU THE MAN? Remember, not the man in the sense of being the Savior, because only one man fits that criterion, but a man willing to go and willing to be a bearer and witness of the Light.

A man's land is the sphere where he operates; his land is his community, it is his neighborhood, it is his street—more specifically—his home. It is where he works, does business, goes to school, where he goes for his recreation. It is the prison where he works, whether as an officer or an inmate. It is his man cave where he watches sports with other men. It is the halfway house he is assigned to as he works on transitioning back into the community, a community he once ravaged with drug dealing, prostitution, murder, and mayhem. In essence, wherever he finds himself, he has to look at it as an opportunity to be God's sent man to that environment. He must not abdicate, nor should he absolve himself of his responsibility to be God's man—God's agent of change and transformation. Because if and when he does, darkness will continue to spread. The serpent will continue to bite.

Where salvation was concerned, the criteria for the God's sent man—the Redeemer, the Savior—would have to be sinless perfection. The human mind must find it difficult to fathom a human being who is without sin. Again, with God the seemingly impossible can be possible. The possibility became a reality when The *Logos*—The Word—became flesh and tabernacled among men. His purpose: to make up the hedge by standing in the gap. First Timothy 2:5 states, "*For there is one God, and one mediator between God and men, the man Christ Jesus.*"

CHAPTER 10

PAPA WAS A ROLLIN' STONE

Wise sayings I heard while growing up have helped me overcome some of the most difficult times and seasons in my life. One such saying is, "a rolling stone gathers no moss." It means a man who does not settle in one place—a man who has very little stability—will find it extremely difficult to achieve success. The man who is a rolling stone is a man who should not be entrusted with certain responsibilities. His lack of commitment—his instability—means the person or persons who depend on him will be disappointed. I use the term "rolling stone" specifically to refer to absentee fathers, especially those who have multiple children with multiple women. There are times in conversation with my wife Paulette when the subject is men with children in different places, and she will remark, "He is the village ram." In my writings, I often make reference to certain songs. Songs have the ability to capture a memory, a time, and a season of life, whether positive or negative. They can also give us a descriptive synopsis of something which impacts us individually or corporately. For music connoisseurs and aficionados, the words,

"Papa was a Rollin' Stone," are easily recognizable as the title of the hit song by the Temptations. The words of this famous song are powerful in their description of men who impregnate different women with no plans on being a committed father to the children. The children who are not aborted come into this world at a disadvantage. For most children, it will impact them negatively because as hard as Momma will work to keep a roof over their heads and food on their table, there are things they need from their father— like teachings on how to become a responsible man. Some men consider it a badge of honor to say, "I have X number of kids with X amount of baby mothers." For a lot of men, child support court, with its ramifications of garnishments, arrests, and suspended driver's licenses has calmed their arrogant boasting.

I feel it is fitting to use some verses of this song to highlight the destructiveness of such behavior, destructive in the sense that fatherlessness can and in many instances will have a negative impact on the abandoned children, on the single mother who bears the burden of caring for the children, and on society if those children become persons with larcenous proclivity.

For full context, let me give you some of the lyrics from, "Papa Was a Rollin' Stone":

It was the third of September
That day I'll always remember, yes I will
'Cause that was the day that my daddy died
I never got a chance to see him
Never heard nothing but bad things about him
Momma, I'm depending on you to tell me the truth
Momma just hung her head and said,
"Son, Papa was a rolling stone
Wherever he laid his hat was his home."

The words of this popular song depict and describe a condition that has ailed the Black community for decades. In no way shape or form am I saying this condition is exclusive to Black families; however, statistics do confirm the high number of single parent households in the Black community with females as head of household. This is the community of which I am a part and that is why I highlight this demographic. I throw no stones in writing this because I too was a rollin' stone at a certain time in my life, when it was fashionable to sleep with as many women as I could. My promiscuous lifestyle led to me fathering multiple children with multiple women—children I was not able to give the quality time, energy, finances, etc. necessary for their proper growth and development. Some were able to overcome my absence in their early years because of the commitment and dedication of their mothers, while others still suffer from the impact today.

The lyrics of the song paint a sad picture of Momma having to hang her head in shame when responding to her child's inquiry about a dead father who was an absentee father when he was alive—a father who was little more than a sperm donor. Equally or more devastating than the momma's response is what the child said, "I never got a chance to see him / Never heard nothing but bad things about him."

Having grown up in a single parent home without my father, and having multiple children with various women allows me to identify with two of the three characters in this song. All of my children have seen me, but I can honestly say that for many years, I was not a good father to them. I was too busy living the street life. I remember calling one of my daughters years ago, and when her mother told her to pick up the phone because it was her father on the line, her response was, "What does he want?" I was hurt, but I understood where she was coming from. I was an absentee father who didn't take or make time for her. On another occasion she asked me a difficult question: Why did I leave her? I did my best to explain to her that I was very immature and irresponsible when I was younger, and that it was no fault of her own. I wasn't making excuses; I was letting her know my mind and life were not at the place at that time to be a committed parent, as shameful as that is and sounds.

I am being transparent about my own shortcomings and failures in describing myself as a rollin' stone in hopes of encouraging men who are estranged and separated from their children. I remember when the mother of one of my daughters told me my daughter had been raped. It was a tough thing to hear, and I felt the guilt of not being there to protect her as a man and as her father. The great thing about being alive is the ability and opportunity to make things right; it may have to start with a phone call, or a letter apologizing for being an absentee father. Your child may not be willing to accept you right away, but at least you will start the ball rolling.

I was watching a program on YouTube in which the host interviews reggae dancehall DJs from a previous era. One of the questions he always asks the interviewee is how many children do you have? A very popular sing-jay (an entertainer who has a hybrid style of delivery that is an amalgamation or combination of blending singing and chanting) said he had around twenty. One of the other questions asked by the host is are you married? Most of his guests readily admit they are not married and have "baby mada" (baby mothers) all over. Interestingly enough, many of them said they came from homes where their fathers had multiple children with different women, which obviously lets me know there is a cycle. The question which has to be asked is who is taking on the responsibility of rearing these children and giving them the love and support they need to grow up to be well adjusted adults? In the case of the entertainer I referred to, and other men in his chosen career, they travel extensively to perform. With a hectic travel schedule any person would be challenged to spend quality time with one or two children, much less twenty. In most instances the children's primary care falls to the mother, grandparents, or other members of the extended family—while the man who planted the seed is off doing his thing. Hence the words of the song from "Papa Was a Rollin' Stone":

> *I never got a chance to see him*
> *Never heard nothing but bad things about him*
> *Momma, I'm depending on you to tell me the truth*
> *Momma just hung her head and said,*
> *"Son, Papa was a rolling stone*
> *Wherever he laid his hat was his home."*

These potent words are an example of a song describing real life events. You can hear the heart of abandoned, neglected children crying out through these words. Momma is the last line of defense against the mental anguish and feelings of abandonment suffered by these children. Momma has to be strong for her children and for herself. When Papa is a rollin' stone, not only are the children impacted—Momma is impacted. She has to deal with rejection, abandonment, physical, mental and emotional stress, and exhaustion from being both Mommy and Daddy to her child(ren). It is unfortunate that many mommas have had to hang their heads when a child raised in a single parent home headed by Momma inquires where is my father? Where is my daddy? Why did Daddy leave? Some of these children grow up maladjusted because they think their father's absence is their fault. Some grow up blaming, rejecting, and even hating their mothers. This is ironic since she is the one who sacrificed and labored to keep the proverbial roof over their heads.

Some daughters wind up with men who impregnate, abuse, and leave them, supposedly for greener pastures, which perpetuates the vicious cycle. If you look at the statistics in cities and communities where there is poverty and its offspring, crime, you will see a high number of households headed by single females. Many of them are not mature in age, emotionally or in other areas needed to care for a child. Please don't blame or scapegoat these women, because in the real world, relationships break up; marriages end, often leaving the children in the care of the mother. With that being said, there is nothing wrong with asking the question, why have multiple children with different men when you are not able to care for them? Both male and females have to exercise discipline and self-control, but I believe the female should even more so because she is the one who runs the risk of getting pregnant. That is the reality. In no way does that absolve a man of his responsibility not to live a reckless lifestyle like Papa in the song.

This is what I believe, and this is personal to me; others have the right to disagree. A child has the best chance to succeed when he or she is brought up in a home where there is a mother and father who love each other—a mother and father who work together to give their child(ren) the kind of home life that will cause them to thrive and prosper. Can children born and raised in a single parent home prosper? Of course, but statistics show they do better with both parents in the home.

THE ROOT IS SLAVERY

The Rollin' Stone mentality and lifestyle has its roots in slavery when the so called master not only sexually violated female slaves who he viewed as his property, he used the Black men—commonly referred to as Bucks—to breed the female slaves like animals in order to produce children to work the fields of the plantation or to be put on the slave auction block. An online article from the site nationalhumanitiescenter.org titled, "On Slaveholders' Sexual Abuse of Slaves: Selections from 19th- & 20th-century Slave Narratives," has this written:

For many enslaved African Americans, one of the cruelest hardships they endured was sexual abuse by the slaveholders, overseers, and other white men and women whose power to dominate them was complete. Enslaved women were forced to submit to their masters' sexual advances, perhaps bearing children who would engender the rage of a master's wife, and from whom they might be separated forever as a result. Masters forcibly paired "good breeders" to produce strong children they could sell at a high price. Resistance brought severe punishment, often death. "I know these facts will seem too awful to relate," warns former slave William J. Anderson in his 1857 narrative, as they are some of the real 'dark deeds' of American Slavery."

A nation or generation who does not know or is unwilling to learn its true history runs the risk of having that history repeated. Hundreds of years later we are still dealing with the effects of slavery, the Jim Crow period, and forces in the media and government who perpetuate a narrative and stereotype of the inferiority of Black people. It is incumbent upon every Black male and female to write our own narrative by the lives we choose to live. We cannot look to outside sources for our complete liberation—we must look within. At a specific time in the past the physical chains of slavery came off, and now it is high time for the mental chains to come off. As the great singer songwriter Robert Nestor Marley sang in "Redemption Song":

"Emancipate yourselves from mental slavery /
None but ourselves can free our minds."

Our success as a people will depend on the strength of the Black family. Men have a vitally important part to play in that success. Some men make an attempt, albeit a futile one, to appease their consciences by giving material things to their children who live outside of their homes. Tangible things are needed, but they cannot replace quality time spent loving and nurturing a child. We don't live in a perfect world, I understand that. Yet there can be no excuse for the kind of promiscuous lifestyle which leaves children exposed, many of them left to fend for themselves at a young age. Some are like the child in the Temptation's song who never saw Daddy, never heard anything but bad things about him—a child who is representative of too many children who have to depend on Momma to fill in the gaps left by Papa.

In the second stanza of the song, Momma tells her child that when Papa died, all he left them was a loan. Papa left them broke and in debt by leaving them a loan, but he also left them exposed by leaving them alone. A sad narrative for far too many families. When a parent dies, the person has to be cremated because there is not enough money for a burial. In other instances, the family is left impoverished because what they used to get from Papa, they receive no more.

In the third stanza of the song, Momma's child said,

Hey, Momma, is it true what they say
That Papa never worked a day in his life?
And Momma, some bad talk going around town

Saying that Papa had three outside children
And another wife and that ain't right
I heard some talk about Papa doing some storefront preaching
Talking about saving souls and all the time leeching
Dealing in debt and stealing in the name of the Lord
Momma just hung her head and said,
"Papa was a rolling stone, my son
Wherever he laid his hat was his home"

Lord, have mercy. Papa was a bigamist, had four recorded children, yet he never worked a day in his life—a bad combination. Then he had the nerve to be preaching; he used the storefront church pulpit to pilfer finances. Papa should not have been preaching; he needed to be delivered. Some of Papa's behavior can be seen in men in the Bible, specifically, Hophni and Phinehas, the sons of the priest Eli. They were supposed to follow in their father's footsteps, but they were two wild brothers. This is what is written about them in 2 Samuel 2:22: "

Now Eli was very old, and heard all that his sons did unto all Israel; and how they lay with the women that assembled at the door of the tabernacle of the congregation." Not only did they sleep with the women, but they also took the portion of the offering which belonged to The Most High for themselves. This is evidence that the promiscuous rollin' stone papas come from all walks of life. Hophni and Phinehas were born into a priestly line, but they were obviously void of Light—like other men who use the church as their harem and personal bank account.

Men who are bearers and witnesses of the Light make the necessary commitment and sacrifice to leave a generational inheritance for their children and grandchildren. First, by leaving a legacy and an example of morality. No man is perfect, but there should be a standard. Along with a legacy and an example of righteous living, they should also leave a tangible inheritance. In other words, they don't leave Momma and the children saddled with debt, alone, and exposed to predatory lenders and creditors seeking to take what little they have. I have never forgotten words of wisdom I heard spoken by a senior mother and grandmother from Jamaica. In her patois vernacular she said, *"Every man have a right fe mine him pickney,"* meaning, it is the right and responsibility of every man to take care of his children. It is extremely difficult and challenging—some would say impossible—for any man who has multiple children by different women in different places to take care of his children effectively, especially when the model or paradigm for care is one which requires quality time to be spent with the child(ren). There isn't much that can give consolation and compensation to children who had a rough time growing up because...

"PAPA WAS A ROLLIN' STONE. WHEREVER HE LAID HIS HAT WAS HIS HOME."

CHAPTER 11

THE HEART OF
THE FATHER

A good father is one of the most unsung, un-praised, unnoticed,
and yet one of the most valuable assets in our society.

—*Billy Graham*

My publisher, mentor, and friend, Mr. Laval Belle, impressed upon me not only how important the title of a book is, but also the importance of the subtitle. My subtitle, *Father, Where Are You?* is important because it correlates a lack of fatherhood with men who are void of Light. The concept of a Father is one that is at the heart of the Bible narrative. From Genesis to Revelation, God Almighty is not pictured and portrayed as some distant cosmic deity; He is referred to as a loving, kind, and merciful Father who cares for His children. Like any good Father, he does discipline His children, but He does it for their benefit.

When someone is hit with an immense tragedy like the sudden loss of a loved one, it is not unusual for the question to be asked, "Why did God allow it to happen?" Some even say, "If there is a God, then why did He allow this to happen?" Some tragedies are so debilitating, they are extremely difficult to deal with mentally and emotionally. For people who trust in God and have faith in Him, it is difficult at times to explain some occurrences. One of our definitions of God is that He is omniscient, meaning He knows all things. He does not know them after the fact, because someone had to tell him; He knows them before they happen. It is very difficult for the natural mind to comprehend how God can know that a tragedy will happen and allow it to happen. This is the reason why we are instructed to, *"Walk by faith and not by sight."* We must trust Him when we cannot see Him.

God was not caught off guard when Adam sinned and caused creation to fall, leaving a void. In His infinite knowledge, He knew it, and planned for it. Sin has many terrible effects, the main one being man's separation from God. Isaiah 59:2 states, *"But your iniquities have separated between you and your God, and your sins have hid his face from you, that he will not hear."* Some people are quick to blame God when a crisis hits but are slow to take responsibility for the sin which separates them from The Almighty.

Everyone in the world is part of God's creation, but the redeemed are called His sons. Sin separates; God redeems and repatriates. Ask Christians to tell you something from the book of Malachi that they have heard church, and they will more than likely quote the verse about robbing God in tithes and offerings and being cursed with a curse. They have heard it read many times in church at offering time. For me, the key chapter and verse in Malachi is not 3:10, but 4:5-6, *"Behold, I will send you Elijah the prophet before the coming of the great and dreadful day of the LORD: And he shall turn the heart of the fathers to the children, and the heart of the children to their fathers, lest I come and smite the earth with a curse."*

This is the crux of the message given to Prophet Malachi by God the Father for His people. Fatherlessness causes young men to act like they are under a curse. When you look at the murder rate in the inner cities of America and other nations of the world, you will see a correlation between murders and other crimes, and households where fathers are either missing or are in the house but not living a lifestyle that is conducive to the proper growth and development of their children. Mothers do an outstanding job with their children, but a son needs his father or some kind of role model of a man who is an asset to his family and community.

Ezekiel was told that God sought a man to make up the hedge and stand in the gap for the land before Him to avert destruction (more on this later). Malachi was told that the heart of the fathers would have to be turned to the children and the children's heart to their fathers for destruction to be averted. Put those two ideas together and what you have is God is looking for men who have the heart of a loving father—men who have the Heart of God. He is looking for fathers who teach their children His ways, to fear and to reverence His name. *"But unto you that fear my name shall the Sun of righteousness arise with healing in his wings; and ye shall go forth, and grow up as calves of the stall"* (Mal. 4:2). The concept of a father and son, or fathers and children is very important. It is one of the reasons Yeshua constantly spoke about and directed the people's attention to His Father in Heaven. He never sought to take credit for the things He did; He was careful to give His Father all the glory. *"Then answered Jesus and said unto them, Verily, verily, I say unto you, The Son can do nothing of himself, but what he seeth the Father do: for what things soever he doeth, these also doeth the Son likewise. For the Father loveth the Son, and sheweth him all things that himself doeth: and he will shew him greater works than these, that ye may marvel"* (Jn. 5:19-20). Jesus had no hidden agenda; His agenda was his assignment from His Father.

There are earthly fathers who chose a life of crime, but I've heard of very few who wanted their son(s) to follow in their footsteps. Their motto is, "Do as I say and not as I do." A good father is not one who is so named biologically, but one who has the characteristics and attributes of the Father of Lights. I was on a prayer line once, and one of the ladies on the line gave an example of Father God as a provider that truly blessed me. She said, "God is not a deadbeat dad; you don't have to take Him to court for support." A man can plant the seed that leads to conception, but it takes a dedicated and committed man to be responsible for taking care of the plant when it is young and tender.

A sterile man cannot impregnate a woman, but he can be a good father to her children. Virile men can become dads, but that does not make them good fathers. There are young men who act out because of anger and bitterness which stems from the fact they miss their fathers, or they have never had a father in their lives. Societies need more mentors who are willing to be surrogate fathers to children who are at risk because they have absentee fathers, whether due to death, abandonment, divorce, or prison. Men void of Light who desire to be delivered from darkness must ask the question, "Father, where are you?" In the same manner, fatherless children are crying out, "Daddy, where are you?" "When are you coming home?" Unfortunately, for many of these children, for many different reasons, Daddy is never coming home as a result of bitter divorce, life in prison, even death.

The idea of the heart of the father is so important, Jesus taught His disciples to start their prayers with the words, "*Our Father, who art in Heaven.*" I made a lot of mistakes as a young husband and father, but it was not until I committed my heart to God my Creator that I learned through His Word what true fatherhood is all about. He is the greatest example because there is no imperfection in Him. Men, if we implement and apply His teachings and instructions in this area, though we won't be perfect, we will be the best fathers we can ever hope to be.

CHAPTER 12

REAL MEN, PLEASE STAND UP

A real man is one who rejects passivity, accepts responsibility, leads courageously, and expects the greater reward, God's reward.
—*Dr. Robert Lewis*

When I was a teenager, there was a popular game show on TV called, *To Tell the Truth,* which the online site Wikipedia (en.wikipedia.org) describes this way,

To Tell the Truth is an American television panel game show in which four celebrity panelists are presented with three contestants and must identify which is the "central character" whose unusual occupation or experience has been read out by the show's moderator/host…The panelists are each given a period of time to question the challengers. Questions are directed to the challengers by number ("Number One," "Number Two," and "Number Three"), with the central character sworn to give truthful answers, and the impostors permitted to lie and pretend to be the central character.

After questioning is complete, each member of the panel votes on which of the challengers they believe to be the central character, either by writing the number on a card or holding up a card with the number of their choice, without consulting the other panelists.

Once the votes are in, the host asks, "Will the real [person's name] please stand up?" The central character then stands, often after some brief playful feinting and false starts among all three challengers.

Please allow me to add a twist to the memorable line in this show and ask, *"Will real men please stand up?!"*

What is a real man? I believe Dr. Robert Lewis' definition that I included at the beginning of the chapter is a great definition. It is not the only a definition, but it is a great place to start. Accepting responsibility and leading courageously beautifully encapsulate what I believe are two key roles of every man. When men abdicate, abandon, or abrogate their roles and responsibility, the ensuing result will be chaos in every stratum of a society. I am not a chauvinist, nor am I a misogynist; women must be empowered to be all The Most High created them to be, but men must not be relegated to second-class citizen status in the institutions of society. If you want to see the danger of an absentee man who is not in his God-given position, go to the book of Genesis chapter 3, specifically, and read about the serpent and the effect his conversation had on Eve, the wife of Adam. The impact is still felt and still being dealt with to this very day. When a man who accepts his Divine responsibility to lead connects with an empowered woman who is willing to work with him, the dynamic duo can and will accomplish great things.

The feminist movement notwithstanding, male leadership does not mean the subjugation, domination, and the control of women. In no way shape or form am I insinuating that abuse of power has not taken place. Real men lead with love and kindness, not with anger and mean spiritedness. Genesis 1:26-28 gives us The Most High's original plan for the man, the woman, and their offspring; both male and female were to have dominion. God was the head, and male and female flowed together in unity. The chaos brought about by the fall meant some structure had to be established until His original mandate could be reestablished. The structure is Christ is the head of the man, and man is the head or covering for the woman. When His structure is not followed, families and society suffer the consequences.

There are women who ran with the feminist movement and went way overboard in asserting their independence. Some had felt powerless for so long, that once they received power through liberation, it intoxicated them. You will hear some of them say, "I don't need a man." Maybe some women do not need a man for some things, but man certainly needs the woman to be who God created her to be in his life. Men who put their trust in God look to His manual, the Bible, for instructions in all things, including the role and responsibility of the male and female. Any other plan put forth by anyone is ungodly, and ungodly plans always yield ungodly results.

Men, if we want prosperous families, we must have an understanding of the role and responsibility of men and women as God intended. We cannot accept worldly models that are opposed to God's Word. We must not discriminate against others, but we must stand firm in defending the institution of family as it was established by The Almighty. We need look no further than the Genesis of things. The Almighty put male and female together so they could help one another in their God-given assignment to take care of the earth. Feminists may not like this, but the Bible is clear, and it says what it says. God created both male and female for His Divine purpose. Feminism is a response to chauvinism and misogyny; however, I don't see anywhere in God's original design where He said women were to be subjugated—kept barefoot and pregnant. I do see where it says she is to have co-dominion with the man. The man and the woman were never designed by their Creator to live and act independently of each other. Families suffer, institutions suffer, and society suffers when they do that. Show me a society where God's design for the man and woman is decimated, denigrated, or destroyed, and I will show you a society that will eventually implode.

> *Like a compass needle that points north, a man's accusing finger always finds a woman. Always.*
>
> —*Khaled Hosseini*

A weak, insecure man points his finger at any and everyone else in order to absolve himself of responsibility for the mess he has created through faulty decision making. A real man will not do that. When he drops the ball, when he falls, he stands up with a spine that is like a metal rod; he will not stay down like he has jelly in his spine. A real man has learned the importance of standing UP for God!

> *Change does not roll in on the wheels of inevitability, but comes through continuous struggle, and so we must straighten our backs and work for our freedom. A man can't ride you unless your back is bent.*
>
> —*Dr. Martin Luther King Jr.*

Real men are not perfect men, they are just men. They will fall at times, but they refuse to wallow in the mud, the muck, and the mire when they have succumbed to a momentary lapse in judgment—a lack of leadership. *"For a just man falleth seven times, and riseth up again: but the wicked shall fall into mischief"* (Prv. 24:16). The wicked are men void of Light—men who need to cry out in repentance, "Father, where are You?"

A real man, the God-man, looks for and chooses the path of peace when he knows he is right, and the other person is wrong. A real man fights to keep his family intact, instead of readily choosing separation and divorce as the easy way out—fighting mentally, emotionally, spiritually, financially, and any other way he has to, to protect his home, his garden, from the serpentine spirits trying to slither in to create a chaotic environment. As darkness covers the earth and gross darkness the people, as human depravity sweeps across societies and people's hearts wax colder and colder, the real men must stand up and take their position of headship and be all God Almighty has called them to be. The United States Army has a slogan which says, "Be all you can be." It is a nice slogan, but real men must be who God called them to be. If you are a real man, stand up now; take a stand for Godliness, for Holiness, for Righteousness, and make an impact for God in your environment.

CHAPTER 13

MAN CAVE OR CAVEMAN? NEANDERTHAL OR CRO-MAGNON?

The ultimate measure of a man is not where he stands in moments of comfort and convenience, but where he stands at times of challenge and controversy.
—Martin Luther King Jr.

I get it! A man needs his space, especially if he is married to or is with a woman who is as clingy as static in your clothes when your skin is dry. He is waiting to exhale and must be given his space, a place to breathe. If that does not happen, there will be a lot of static in the relationship. He loves and adores his queen, but she must honor and respect his need for "him" time—a place to retreat for solitude. The term "man cave" has become very popular. He retreats there in order to be alone or to spend time with other males who need a temporary respite from the vicissitudes of a life which at times can be overwhelming.

What a person does in his or her spare time reflects how they think and feel. There is nothing wrong with extracurricular activities like sports or video games. A problem occurs when football, baseball, basketball, video games, or hanging out with the fellas becomes more time-consuming than prayer, fasting, and studying God's Word and family time. What goes in will come out. *"A good man out of the good treasure of his heart bringeth forth that which is good; and an evil man out of the evil treasure of his heart bringeth forth that which is evil: for of the abundance of the heart his mouth speaketh"* (Lk. 6:45).

If hours are spent during the week and on weekends in front of a TV, a computer screen, or a game console for the purpose of entertainment for soul stimulation, an over-indulgence in Madden will cause a man's relationship to become maddening. The video game console cannot console and give comfort in a difficult, challenging situation. Watching football can and will excite, incite, and stimulate the brain, causing the release of dopamine; as a result, a habitual craving for such activities can develop. Where there is a lack of balance in a marriage, because the man spends too much time in isolation in his man cave, tensions will arise.

According to an online article on the website healthline.com which was medically reviewed by Timothy J. Legg, PhD, PsyD, on November 5, 2019, and written by Ann Pietrangelo:

Dopamine is a neurotransmitter made in the brain. Basically, it acts as a chemical messenger between neurons. Dopamine is released when your brain is expecting a reward. When you come to associate a certain activity with pleasure, mere anticipation may be enough to raise dopamine levels. It could be a certain food, sex, shopping, or just about anything else that you enjoy. For example, suppose your "go-to" comfort food is homemade double chocolate chip cookies. Your brain may increase dopamine when you smell them baking or see them come out of the oven. When you eat them, the flood of dopamine acts to reinforce this craving and focus on satisfying it in the future.

Merciful Father, help the man who feeds his brain with pornography, the man in the cave whose brain has an insatiable appetite for the reward and pleasure of porn, which he has made an integral part of his entertainment buffet—buffeting his mind with a smorgasbord of erotica. With the explosion of technology, like the Internet, cell phones, and other portable, handheld devices like tablets, a man can receive soul and flesh stimulation twenty-four/seven.

The true man of God is disciplined in how, when, where, and to what he allocates his precious time. He does not over consume entertainment, which causes soul stimulation. His place of retreat is not a lair or a place to hone caveman-like appetites and inclinations by various machinations. A secular man may need a man cave, but the man of God needs a prayer closet, a meditation room—a place and space where he can spend quality time communing with his Creator. When he exits that place and space, he brings something from the presence of The Almighty which will edify, exhort, and equip the people around him.

He refuses to allow his private place and space to become a mini house within the larger house, reducing him and his wife to roommates instead of spiritual soul mates. He uses his retreat to spend time gleaning in the presence of the Lord—receiving wisdom, knowledge, and understanding on how to become a better man, husband, and father. A man who makes an impact by leaving a Kingdom print in the sphere God has called him to influence. In so doing, he is not MIA (missing in action), neither is he AWOL (absent without leave). He is a spiritual soldier of the Kingdom whose hands his Creator has taught to war for his family, to war for his community, to war for the downtrodden and the brokenhearted.

When attacks are being launched left, right, and center, he does not retreat; he does not surrender. He does not respond from a soulish, carnal place because he understands that he *"Wrestles not against flesh and blood, but against principalities, against powers, against the rulers of the darkness of this world, against spiritual wickedness in high places."* With such an understanding, he is suited and booted for war from the top of his head to the soles of his feet with the whole armor of God. For the secular, unsaved man void of Light, the man cave is a place where lascivious and licentious activities are done and hidden. It's a place that facilitates destruction, not construction. I heard a notable Spanish saying a long time ago which states, "Tiempo es oro." It means time is gold; time is precious so it must be spent well.

Men, we all have time. As for me, I never spent mine wisely or precisely. Living recklessly BC (before Christ), I didn't live a life of giving. When I did give, there were strings attached, causing me to become cold, uncaring, and detached. But when Christ became Lord in my life,

> *I threw the old man overboard, like the mariners did when Jonah was on board / the ship, don't trip / A prophetic man whose rebellion caused him to be a pathetic man / on the run— no one chased him with a gun / he refused to share true discipleship with Nineveh / because he thought they were criminal.*
>
> —*Fidel Donaldson*

Man cave or caveman? Neanderthal or Cro-Magnon? I've been known to wax poetic at times. The cave man is brutish. He rules with a club and has the "barefoot and pregnant" mentality when it comes to the treatment of women—a mindset which says,

"It's my way or the highway." That is the reason some women chose the highway instead of his way after suffering silently for many years, suffering with a gruff and tough man who morphed into a hybrid of King Kong and Godzilla. The honey left the moon real fast. "Honey-do" became, "Honey, I can't." During the wooing and courting phase, he pretended to be a gentleman, but how quickly he morphed into a caveman—a neanderthal and a Cro-Magnon man. It didn't take long for the honey to jump out of the moon causing him to become what DJ Shabba Ranks called, "A Bedroom Bully." Both male and female were created in the Image and Likeness of God which means His Image and Likeness have the components of strength and compassion. God's man must reflect His versatility—strong in leadership, yet meek, gentle, kind, and loving when a situation requires it.

It is extremely difficult for some men to adopt such a posture. They believe meekness is a sign of weakness. Their idea of manliness is the macho man. It's not so with a man of Light. He is not swayed easily by the opinions of others. He endeavors to please, to be like His Maker. When a man looks at his private space as a retreat for prayer and communion, he will think and act like the One he prays to, the One he retreated to commune with. Please don't get me wrong. I'm not saying only cavemen hang out in man caves, but I do believe words have power. Names are given to reflect the attributes of the person or thing that is named—there is a reason you don't come across men with the name Judas.

There are multiple references to caves in the Bible. When a man went to a cave, it was to hide or be hidden. Most of the time they were hiding in fear because their lives were in danger. The first time the word is used in the Bible is in the book of Genesis in reference to Lot. After the angels rescued him from the destruction of Sodom, they told him to escape to a certain mountain. He refused to escape to the mountain fearing evil and death overtaking him. When an angel is sent by God Almighty to rescue you and he instructs you to escape to a mountain, I don't see how evil and death could overtake you. Fear causes a man to settle for a low place when God sends him to a high place. Instead of the mountain, Lot settled for a place called Zoar, which means, "a little place; to be small, that is, (figuratively) ignoble: be brought low." Fear will cause you to think small and act small, until you eventually become small. The thing about letting fear rule you is it allows you to have no rest, nor does it allow you to have peace. "

And Lot went up out of Zoar, and dwelt in the mountain, and his two daughters with him; for he feared to dwell in Zoar: and he dwelt in a cave, he and his two daughters" (Gen. 19:30).

It was in the cave that his daughters got him drunk and lay with him. Out of their incestuous liaison with him in his drunken stupor, two sons—Ammon and Moab—were conceived and birthed. Nothing good can come out of you if you are in your man cave consuming alcohol and partaking in perversion.

There was a God-fearing man who was governor in the house of Ahab by the name of Obadiah. When Jezebel killed the prophets of the LORD, this great man hid a hundred and fifty of them in a cave. While they were there, he fed them with bread and water. When a cave is used for a noble purpose as it was with Obadiah, it is a good thing. When a man is hiding out in his man cave feeding his flesh, that is a bad thing.

Elijah was one of Yahweh's great prophets. After defeating the prophets of Baal, Jezebel put a hit on his life. Ahab was weak, but Jezebel was no joke; she was a tough cookie. Her threat was intimidating enough to cause Elijah to flee. He left his servant at Beer-sheba and he went on a day's journey into the wilderness, where he sat under a juniper tree desiring to die. While sleeping under the juniper tree, he had an angelic visitation that strengthened him. When he left from under the tree, he traveled for forty days and forty nights until he came to Horeb, the Mount of God. He found a cave there and lodged in it.

It was there that the Word of the LORD came to him. God didn't ask him how he was feeling or if was he okay. God asked him, *"What are you doing here, Elijah?"* Since God is omniscient, the question was rhetorical, similar to when He asked, *"Adam, where art thou?"* In other words, *"Why are you hiding from me?"* In Elijah's case, the question was asked for him to think about his purpose. He was called and sent to execute the plan of Yahweh. Instead of doing so, he was in a cave, and judging by his response, he was not in a good place or space—mentally or emotionally. Men! Do not hide in a cave when you should be out executing The Almighty's plan, especially after He visited you when you were under the juniper tree despairing of life, wanting to die, and you've had an angelic visitation which strengthened you.

When Elijah responded to God, he didn't talk about dying—he told God how jealous he had been for Him. Then Elijah pointed the finger at the people, accusing them of forsaking the Covenant, throwing down His altars, and slaying His prophets with the sword. He sounded paranoid when He told Yahweh: "

And I, even I only, am left; and they seek my life, to take it away" (1 Kgs. 19:10). Men, you will feel lonely on the journey at times, but you are not alone. Please don't throw a pity party; God is not going to attend. He is merciful and full of compassion, but He is about His business. He called His prophet to stand upon the mount before Him so he could feel His presence passing by. I believe Yah did it to remind Elijah that he needed not fear for his life. God didn't go into the cave; He called him out. Elijah came and stood at the entrance to the cave to receive instructions. God didn't tell him to take some time off from his prophetic assignment; He sent him back through the wilderness to anoint his replacement and to anoint the man who would put an end to the shenanigans of Jezebel. My friend and brother Attorney Michael Valentine said, "God fired him." I'm going to cut Elijah some slack and say God sent him to anoint his replacement so he could take him to Heaven in a chariot of fire.

If you choose to be in your man cave, your prison cell, in solitary confinement, or shut up in your room with the lights out and the curtains drawn, wallowing in self-pity, that is up to you. God has already hand-picked your replacement, and He will use you to anoint and mentor him. Whether in the cave or another place, come out! Come out, wherever you are! Rise Up! STAND UP!

CHAPTER 14

A MAN SENT FROM GOD

Also, I heard the voice of the Lord, saying, Whom shall I send, and who will go for us? Then said I, Here am I; send me.

—Isaiah 6:8

The Bible does not say God sent a white man, a Black man, a Spanish man, or an Asian man; not a rich man, a poor man, or an educated man—simply, "There was a man sent from God." Not a superman, but a man chosen by God before the foundation of the world for one of the greatest assignments given to any man.

With the feminization of so many men, it is vitally important to state emphatically, unequivocally, and assertively: GOD SENT A MAN. Nowadays when speaking about men, the word has to be qualified with the term, "a real man." There is a segment of the population who prefer to be described as agender people ("a" meaning "without"); they are also called genderless, gender-free, or non-gendered. They identify themselves as having no gender or being without a gender identity. When God formed man and created woman, there was no ambiguity concerning their gender or how they should function in the world as two people created in His Image and Likeness. God's sent man does not suffer from an identity crisis. He is not confused about who he is. His manhood is not threatened by shifting secular societal norms of what manhood should be.

A man who struggles with his identity is like a rudderless ship that is tossed to and fro with every wind and wave. Men must be firm in their understanding of who God created them to be. In the entertainment industry and other places in society, there are males wearing dresses and skirts, dyeing and styling their hair like women, piercing both ears and other parts of their bodies, putting makeup on, and probably wearing women's underwear. If God Almighty created you to be a man, then you should think and act like the man created by God. The norms and mores of societies shift based on people's whims and fancies, but God does not change and neither does His Word. Both God and His Word are immutable. Men cannot and should not attempt to twist the Word to suit their desire to reinvent themselves—to live lifestyles pleasing to their human nature, but abhorrent to God.

John the Baptist's birth was the fulfillment of the words spoken to Prophet Malachi by God. John came in the spirit of Elijah to prepare the way for the Lord—the Lord who would reconcile and return the hearts of the fathers to the children and the hearts of the children to the fathers. A real man sent by God does not only prepare his own way, but he also prepares the way for others. The angel Gabriel visited the priest Zacharias to inform him that his wife Elisabeth would conceive and birth a son. Zacharias and Elisabeth had prayed for years for a son; Elisabeth was barren, and by the time Zacharias had the angelic visitation, they were both old. Gabriel told him to name his son John and informed him of the things he would do for the Lord and for His people.

According to Wikipedia: "John" is a theophoric name originating from the Hebrew name וְחָנִי (*Yôḥānān*), or in its longer form וְנָחֹהִי (*Yəhôḥānān*), meaning "YHWH has been gracious."

Zacharias was told his son John would bring joy to him and his wife, and many would rejoice at his birth. He would be great in the sight of the Lord; most of all, he would be filled with the *Ruach* (Holy Spirit). Men who are sent by God should be a joy, not only to their friends and family, but also to the people they come in contact with. The joy they bring flows from the indwelling of the Holy Spirit. John's life would cause many of the children of Israel to turn to the Lord their God. Many, according to the Bible, but not all, because there are some people who will not turn to God. The scripture that describes his assignment is what motivated me to write this book. The first time I read it, it left an indelible impression on my heart. It left a mark that could not be removed because it revealed to me the purpose of every man who is chosen and sent by God.

> *There was a man sent from God, whose name was John. He was sent to bear witness of the light.*
>
> —*John 1:6*

He was a bold man, but he was a humble man. His humility shone in the fact that he felt unworthy to baptize the Lamb of God. When John came to the Jordan to baptize the people, he told them, "*He it is, who coming after me is preferred before me, whose shoe's latchet I am not worthy to unloose*" (Jn. 1:27). He described himself as the voice of one crying in the wilderness. His assignment: to make straight the way of the Lord, in fulfillment of the words spoken by the prophet Esaias (Isaiah).

John was not dressed in the fine apparel of nobility, neither did he dine succulently on high priced foods. His clothing was made of camel's hair, he wore a leather girdle about his loins, and his meat was locusts and wild honey (Mt. 3:4). His primary focus was not the food that went into his belly, nor was it the clothes he wore on his body—it was the God who sent him, and the people and the Savior to whom he was sent. Men sent from God carry themselves in a dignified manner in terms of their apparel; they recognize their bodies are temples where His Spirit dwells. They are not shallow. Their identity, value, and self-worth are not tied to external things. Like John, they are driven by their call and their assignment.

When John came on the scene preaching the gospel of the Kingdom—more specifically, preaching repentance for entrance into the Kingdom—the people had not heard the prophetic voice in over four hundred years. The period between Malachi and Matthew is called the Intertestamental Period. John's voice would be the first authentic prophetic voice the people had heard in a very long time.

His motivation was not an offering; it was not to get a building to start a church—he was preaching for souls. He was preaching to get the people to turn from vain religion, from having a form of godliness, yet not having hearts which were turned to God. The people were in that condition because the leaders had attached a lot of things to the law which caused them to be in bondage. John's ministry represented a *kairos*—a paradigm shifting moment. People from Jerusalem, Judea, and all the regions around Jordan came to be baptized and to repent of their sins. This is the effect Holy Spirit filled men sent from God have. They don't have to use trickery to get people's attention.

John did not mince his words when he saw many of the Pharisees and Scribes coming to be baptized. They came because they recognized the authenticity of God's call on his life. He called them a generation of vipers—a stinging rebuke and criticism of them by God's prophet. He told them, *"Bring forth therefore fruits meet for repentance"* (Mt. 3:8). The Amplified Bible says it this way: *"So produce fruit that is consistent with repentance [demonstrating new behavior that proves a change of heart, and a conscious decision to turn away from sin]."*

God's sent man desires to see fruit borne in the lives of the people he is sent to. He has no problem calling out the religious establishment if it is the cause of people being in bondage.

CHAPTER 15

BEARER AND WITNESS OF THE LIGHT

It is during our darkest moment that
we must focus to see the light.

—Aristotle

I magine a world where there is no light, a world where the sun does not shine, and the moon does not exist. It is hard to imagine since human beings have never had to live without light. Even in impoverished countries where some communities are without electricity, the sun gives light for the day and the moon gives light for the night. From Genesis to Revelation, the Bible instructs us about the importance of light, especially as it is opposed to darkness. The first recorded words we have in the Bible from God reference light, *"And God said, Let there be light: and there was light"* (Gen. 1:3). God spoke light into being because the earth was without form; it was void and darkness was upon the face of the deep. God is awesome in His splendor and in His majesty and in His creative ability. Man has to harness electricity, enclose it in a bulb or some other casing in order to have light. God spoke light into being and put darkness in its place.

The simple statement that God created Heaven and the earth is one of the most challenging concepts confronting the modern mind. The vast galaxy we live in is spinning at the incredible speed of 490,000 miles an hour, but even at this breakneck speed, our galaxy still needs 200 million years to make one rotation. And there are over one billion other galaxies in the universe. Second Peter 3:8 states,

"But, beloved, be not ignorant of this one thing, that one day is with the Lord as a thousand years, and a thousand years as one day." Mind boggling and awe inspiring; no wonder Job had this to say about God: *"Which alone spreadeth out the heavens, and treadeth upon the waves of the sea. Which maketh Arcturus, Orion, and Pleiades, and the chambers of the south. Which doeth great things past finding out; yea, and wonders without number"* (Job 9:8-10). The light He caused to manifest as recorded in Genesis 1:3 was not from the sun nor the moon because He had not created them when He said, *"Let there be light."* He created the sun and the moon as great lights to rule the day and the night. He also created stars. An online article on the website apologeticspress.org, written by Eric Lyons, M.Min. concurs with this assertion.

On day one God made intrinsic light; on day four He made the generators of light. Keep in mind that "the Father of lights" (James 1:17), who is "light" (1 John 1:5), could create light easily without first having to create the Sun, Moon, and stars. Just as God could produce a fruit-bearing tree on day three without a seed, He could produce light supernaturally on day one without the "usual" light bearers (which subsequently were created on day four). Again, there is no indication in Scripture that the generators of light already were made before day four.

Dr. R.C. Sproul (pronounced "Sprowl") gave this example of God's might and His omnipotence in creation:

I sat in terrified silence the first day of my freshman class in astronomy. The professor posed a question for us: "Suppose that we have a scale where an inch equals a million miles. How far would it be to the nearest star apart from our sun? Would it be one hundred feet? Three hundred feet? Or five hundred feet? My mind began to calculate frantically. Twelve inches make one foot. One foot then would mean twelve million miles. Multiply that by one hundred and the first option meant a distance of over a billion miles.

Now, I knew that our sun was ninety-three million miles from the earth. It seemed reasonable that the next nearest star would not be much more than ten times that distance, so I guessed one hundred feet was the correct answer. I was wrong. So were all the other students who guessed either three hundred feet or five hundred feet. The professor fooled us. He said, "None of the above." He went on to explain that the nearest star was approximately the distance from Pittsburgh to Chicago with each inch equaling a million miles. He gave us a little more help.

"Light travels at a rate of 186,000 miles per second. That is, in one second light can travel seven-and-a-half times around the earth. The light that we see twinkling at night from the nearest star left that star on its way to Earth four-and-a-half years ago!" The distance from earth to the nearest star is four-and-a-half light years away. Traveling at a speed of 186,000 miles per second it takes over four years to reach us! I could not fathom such immensity.

I concur wholeheartedly with Dr. Sproul; my mind cannot grasp such magnitude. I wrote all of that concerning light as a pretext to explain the key, yet not the only purpose for God sending the man John. It is the purpose that should define every man God has called out of darkness into His marvelous Light. A man must first understand God's purpose for his life, then he must be willing to yield his will to God so He can manifest Divine Purpose. Yeshua understood His purpose at twelve years old. He never lost focus or sight of that purpose. When he was the age of twelve, His parents could not find Him on their return from a pilgrimage to Jerusalem. After searching for three days, they found Him in the temple in Jerusalem, sitting in the midst of doctors, both hearing them and asking them questions.

> *And when they saw him, they were amazed: and his mother said unto him, Son, why hast thou thus dealt with us? behold, thy father and I have sought thee sorrowing. And he said unto them, How is it that ye sought me? wist ye not that I must be about my Father's business?*
>
> *—Luke 2:48-49*

Men sent from God spend time in the temple teaching and learning. They put the business of the Kingdom at the forefront of all they say and do. In times of extreme difficulty, they let their Light shine. They refuse to forsake His purpose for their lives. In the Garden of Gethsemane Yeshua asked Father God to let the cup pass, if it were possible. Then He said, *"Not my will but Thine be done."* A man who is unwilling to submit his Will to God is a man who will not be used by God. There is no one who knows what is best for a man like the One who created him. In the earthly realm, who knows a child better than his parents? If earthly parents have the best knowledge of their children, then Abba Father must have the best knowledge about His children. He knows them best because He created them in His Image and in His Likeness.

John, the beloved disciple, said the purpose of Jesus manifesting was that He might destroy the works of the devil. John the Baptist was Jesus' predecessor—the preparer of the way for the ministry of Jesus. John didn't act like he was the Light but pointed the people of his day to the Light—the Lamb of God who taketh away the sins of the world. It is the responsibility of every man sent by God to point people to the Light. We do that first by letting our Light shine. When we come in contact with people who are in darkness, they must see the Light through our words and deeds. Most importantly, they most know who the source of the Light is. He is the One Apostle Peter referred to as the day star: *"We have also a more sure word of prophecy; whereunto ye do well that ye take heed, as unto a light that shineth in a dark place, until the day dawn, and the day star arise in your hearts"* (2 Pet. 1:19).

John received the baptism of Holy Spirit when he was in his mother's womb. From that moment he was empowered by God and set aside to be the preparer of the way for the Messiah, the bearer and witness of the Light.

John 1:6-9 says this about him: *"There was a man sent from God, whose name was John. The same came for a witness, to bear witness of the Light, that all men through him might believe. He was not that Light, but was sent to bear witness of that Light. That was the true Light, which lighteth every man that cometh into the world."*

The word, "witness" is the Greek word *marturia* (pronounced "mar-too-ree¢-ah"), and it means, "evidence given, a record, or a testimony." From the root word *martus* (pronounced "mar¢-toos"), it's where we get the old English words "martir" or "martyr." As a noun, Merriam-Webster's Dictionary defines a martyr as, "a person who voluntarily suffers death as the penalty of witnessing to and refusing to renounce a religion: a person who sacrifices something of great value and especially life itself for the sake of principle."

As Christians, we should describe ourselves as being in a covenant relationship with Abba Father, and not a religion. The principles we should be willing to lay everything down for—including our lives—are the principles of God's Kingdom found in the Holy Scriptures. Being a witness of the Light is both precious and priceless. God's mercy allowed us to be delivered from darkness to be witnesses of His Light. The ultimate purpose of light is to dispel darkness. The works of the devil are shrouded and cloaked in darkness, and so are the works of the men he has bound. Apostle Paul wrote,

"But if our gospel be hid, it is hid to them that are lost: In whom the god of this world hath blinded the minds of them which believe not, lest the light of the glorious gospel of Christ, who is the image of God, should shine unto them" (2 Cor. 4:3-4).Before the fall, Adam had no need of a mediator to stand between him and God. After the fall, mankind needed a mediator because of separation. Christ is the One and only reconciler. When the *Logos* became flesh, He allowed man to see what the Image of God looked like. Sin had perverted the image and likeness of man, so the Savior came to restore him. The Image and Likeness of Almighty God in Christ is glorious Light. No man can see God and live, so God the Word cloaked Himself in the person of Christ so man could see the Light. Sin blinds the eyes, but Christ is the Light who shines bright for all mankind to see. Eyes that are blind are eyes that cannot see the Light. The gospel of Christ, also called the Good News—the Word of God—is Light. In that sense, Light is revelatory knowledge, information, from God that casts out darkness.

A man who lacks understanding of God's principles is a man who lives in darkness. The principles of God must govern every facet of a man's life. In every area of a man's life he must ask himself the pertinent question, "Am I a BEARER AND WITNESS OF DIVINE LIGHT?" Not simply someone who sees and hears

Him through His Word, prayer, fasting, and worship—but someone willing to sacrifice so other men can be delivered and become His witnesses also.

Yeshua told His disciples that as long as He was in the world, He was the Light of the World. The Bible instructs us to be in the world but not of the world. What happened when He rose from the grave and ascended to the Right Hand of the Throne of God? Was the land plunged into utter darkness?

Here is something important that I have to write about the crucifixion of Christ. *"And when the sixth hour was come, there was darkness over the whole land until the ninth hour"* (Mk. 15:33).

Using Gematria (an alphanumeric code of assigning a numerical value to a name, word, or phrase based on its letters) to examine this verse, six is the number of Satan and represents the carnality of man, while nine is the number of the Holy Spirit. Satan and carnality are manifested in darkness, but the Holy Spirit illuminates with Light. The fulfillment of the promise Christ gave His disciples is what kept darkness from consuming the world.

"And, behold, I send the promise of my Father upon you: but tarry ye in the city of Jerusalem, until ye be endued with power from on high" (Lk. 24:49). They were saddened when He told them it was expedient for them that He went away. The prospect of Him leaving would cause anyone to sorrow—his mother and father sorrowed when they could not find Him for three days. Anyone who does not have Him in their life will sorrow in this life and in the life to come. I am not suggesting that Christians are happy and full of joy all the time, but He gives us peace in the midst of the storm. He teaches us how to joy in tribulation. He told His disciples if He did not go, the Comforter would not come. Sending the Comforter would fulfill the promise. The Comforter is the Holy Spirit. He illuminates the life of every disciple of Christ. He was in Christ without measure. That is why He was able to say:

"The prince of this world cometh, and hath nothing in me" (Jn. 14:30).

When the prince of this world comes to tempt you—and he will—what will he find? Will he find the glorious Light of the Messiah shining in what you say and do, or will he find masturbation, fornication, adultery, lying, cheating, stealing, and scheming? Let him find the Light, and when he does, he will flee. Any area of a man's life that is not submitted to God is an area where the enemy has legal right to operate. The only hope for that man is found in these words, *"Submit yourselves therefore to God. Resist the devil, and he will flee from you"* (Jas. 4:7).

So, the church, which is made up of blood-washed believers in whom the Holy Spirit dwells, is the reflector of the Light of Christ to the world. When the church's Light is hidden, the world is a very dark place. Yeshua's words to His disciples confirm this,

Ye are the light of the world. A city that is set on an hill cannot be hid. Neither do men light a candle, and put it under a bushel, but on a candlestick; and it giveth light unto all that are in the house. Let your light so shine before men, that they may see your good works, and glorify your Father which is in heaven.

—Matthew 5:14-16

When the Light of God shines radiantly through us in word and deed, men who are convicted will turn from darkness unto His marvelous Light. As men we must make sure we are doing what He saved us to do—bear witness of the Light. In every area and stratum of life, we must drive away darkness. God's sent man must never be the source of darkness. If he falls and becomes the source, then he must repent immediately so his Light can continue to shine.

A man can find himself in very dark environments at various times in his life. A prison can be a very dark place. If you come to know the True Light, Yeshua ha-Mashiach, in a prison, then it is your duty and responsibility as a citizen and an ambassador of Yahweh's Kingdom to be the bearer and witness of His Light in that dark environment. This does not mean you allow people to walk over you because they think you are a punk, or you are soft; it does mean you do everything that you can to shine the Light so others can see it and be transformed. Your spirit, mind, soul, and body belong to Yah, so they must not be used for perverted thoughts and actions. For this reason, the Christian Soldier who lives behind the prison wall must be extremely disciplined. He must mortify the deeds of the flesh because no good thing dwelleth therein.

I remember growing up and hearing my mom say, "Turn off the lights." She was asking us not to run up the light bill unnecessarily. We used to have light bulbs that had different wattages. A watt is the amount of energy a light bulb uses. The lower the watt, the lower the electric bill. We had thirty-, sixty-, and one-hundred-watt bulbs. In order to reduce the light bill, my mom would use a sixty-watt bulb instead of a one-hundred-watt bulb. There is a distinct difference between darkness and gross darkness. Darkness requires a certain level of light to dispel it, and gross darkness requires greater light. In your home you don't need the kind of flood lights that are used in a stadium for a night game. Your home would be bright, but the light would blind you, defeating the purpose of having the light. God Almighty dwells in perfect Light. Yeshua is the full expression and manifestation of Divine Light in bodily form: *"For God, who commanded the light to shine out of darkness, hath shined in our hearts, to give the light of the knowledge of the glory of God in the face of Jesus Christ"* (2 Cor. 4:6). From the Hebrew perspective, the heart (*leb*) represents the center of the man. It is sad that the first time the word heart is mentioned in the Bible, it is about the wickedness in man. According to Genesis 6:5-6, "

And God saw that the wickedness of man was great in the earth, and that every imagination of the thoughts of his heart was only evil continually. And it repented the Lord that he had made man on the earth, and it grieved him at his heart." Notice the connection between man's thoughts and his heart; this is because "heart" refers to man's mind, to his understanding. Since thought precedes action, a man's actions will be based on the way he thinks, and on the things that influence his mind.

Hence, Proverbs 23:7, *"For as he thinketh in his heart, so is he: Eat and drink, saith he to thee; but his heart is not with thee."*

The Light God called forth when the earth was dark is the Light that shines in the heart every man who is submitted to the Lordship of Jesus Christ. This Light is the Light of His Glory. This Light eliminates the darkness of ignorance by giving man the knowledge of the glory of God. Prophet Isaiah prophesied about this glorious Light when he said:

Arise, shine; for thy light is come, and the glory of the Lord is risen upon thee. For, behold, the darkness shall cover the earth, and gross darkness the people: but the Lord shall arise upon thee, and his glory shall be seen upon thee. And the Gentiles shall come to thy light, and kings to the brightness of thy rising.

—Isaiah 60:1-3

Christ is the Light sent by Yahweh to shine in the hearts of Gentiles.

There's no such thing as the light at the end of the tunnel, you must realize that you are the light.

—Anonymous

CHAPTER 16

PUT SOME WOOD ON THE FIRE

Every man must decide whether he will walk in the light of creative altruism or in the darkness of destructive selfishness.

—*Martin Luther King Jr.*

A gain, darkness, which is synonymous with evil, is always seeking an entry point to a man's heart, his mind, his life. *"Give no place to the devil"* (Eph. 4:27). If you give him some space, he will take over and be your landlord. If you are a Christian man who goes to the strip club to get sexual gratification from scantily clad women dancing on stage around a pole; if you stick money in their underwear while they are gyrating on your lap, then you are contributing to the darkness of the world. When you are in the club partaking in the activities, your Light is not shining—you are in darkness like the rest of the patrons. When you are up at night looking at pornography and other erotic material—you are adding to the darkness that is in the world. *"Wherewithal shall a young man cleanse his way? by taking heed thereto according to thy word* (Ps. 119:9).

My wife and I were watching a documentary recently about a man who had multiple sclerosis (MS). He refused to accept that there was no cure. His father was a researcher who spent a great deal of time researching information about MS and found out that people who lacked vitamin D in their bodies and ate a lot of foods that were not nutritious were more likely to contract MS. He shared the information with his son who started taking vitamin D and launched a campaign to bring awareness to his father's findings. When the son adopted a strict diet of healthy eating, taking vitamin D, and exercise, his body was strengthened against the ravages of the disease.

In an online article titled, "The Sun is Your Best Source of Vitamin D," found on healthline.com, written by Ryan S. Ramans, MS, RD, on April 18, 2018, had this to say about vitamin D:

> *When your skin is exposed to sunlight, it makes vitamin D from cholesterol. The sun's ultraviolet B (UVB) rays hit cholesterol in the skin cells, providing the energy for vitamin D synthesis to occur. Vitamin D has many roles in the body and is essential for optimal health. Photosynthesis is the process by which green plants and some other organisms use sunlight to synthesize foods from carbon dioxide and water. Photosynthesis in plants generally involves the green pigment chlorophyll and generates oxygen as a byproduct.*

In the same manner that sunlight facilitates photosynthesis in green plants and other organisms, the children of God use "Son-Light" from Yeshua, the Son of Righteousness, to get our spiritual nourishment.

Men sent from God are empowered to witness because they walk in the Light. They are energized by the Light. Like John the Baptist, when they witness and let their Light shine, people will believe in Yashua. They will call on His name and they will be saved. He said He is the Light of the World, and that means true spiritual enlightenment can come from no other source. There can be pseudo light but no true Light outside of Him. Believers know this because it is written in the Scriptures, *"And no marvel; for Satan himself is transformed into an angel of light. Therefore, it is no great thing if his ministers also be transformed as the ministers of righteousness; whose end shall be according to their works"* (2 Cor. 11:14-15).

I believe all of the world's religions have some truth in them, but there is a difference between some truth, and **the** truth. Jesus said He is, *"The way, the truth, and the life; no man cometh to the Father, but by me."* The reason being, the Father dwells in unapproachable Light. When Moses came down from the mountain where he was given the Ten Commandments, his face shone because of his exposure to the brightness of the glorious Light; the people could not stand the glare, so Moses' face had to be veiled. With His death, burial, and His resurrection, YESHUA rent the veil which separated man from the Holy of Holies—the place where Almighty God's presence resided in the temple. Now, the redeemed can come boldly before the throne to find help, and to obtain mercy in time of need. We are not destroyed when we approach the throne because God does not see us in a sinful state, but through the blood shed by the sacrifice Jesus made. He is not only the way, the truth, and the life—He is also the way, the truth, and He is the Light. The Light which shineth in the souls of the redeemed. The Light that allows the redeemed man to walk in sanctification and consecration.

A man is not the head of his house simply because he is stronger than the woman; he is not the head because he brings home the bread (money). He is the head because his headship is the order established by his Creator, God. As the head there are many hats that are worn by the man—Protector and Provider are two of many. One of man's most important role is as the PRIEST of his home. As the high priest of his home, he has the responsibility of setting the tone and the atmosphere for strengthening his family in the things of God. His wife has the responsibility of working with him, but he is the pacesetter. His role as priest of the home for his wife and children is so important, God made sure Moses informed the people of it.

> *Therefore, shall ye lay up these my words in your heart and in your soul, and bind them for a sign upon your hand, that they may be as frontlets between your eyes. And ye shall teach them your children, speaking of them when thou sittest in thine house, and when thou walkest by the way, when thou liest down, and when thou risest up. And thou shalt write them upon the doorposts of thine house, and upon thy gates: That your days may be multiplied, and the days of your children, in the land which the Lord sware unto your fathers to give them, as the days of heaven upon the earth.*
>
> *—Deuteronomy 11:18-21*

It was the head's—the priest's—responsibility to make sure the Word of God, the Light, permeated the house and all who dwelt therein. Obedience on the part of the priest would cause their days to be multiplied so that Heaven would manifest on earth. Those instructions were given under the Old Covenant, but the New Testament confirms the fact that men and women are priests of The Most High God. Times and seasons may change, but the responsibility of the priest remains—keeping the Light burning in the temple, in the tabernacle, in the house:

"But ye are a chosen generation, a royal priesthood, an holy nation, a peculiar people; that ye should shew forth the praises of

him who hath called you out of darkness into his marvellous light"
(1 Pt. 2:9). When the Lord established the priesthood, Moses
was instructed to make robes of glory and beauty for Aaron
and his sons. The purpose was so they could minister to Him
in the priest's office. The first responsibility of the priest in the
home is to minister to Him, then to his family. The man has to
spend time in intimate ministry to God. The New Testament
priest does not need outer garments for glory and beauty like
Aaron and his sons because they have inner beauty and glory
through the indwelling of God's Holy Spirit. The first priests
were instructed by God to never allow the fire on the altar in the
temple to go out; God's instructions have not changed. Every
man sent by God to be a priest of his home must keep the fire
burning; he must keep the Light shining.

> *And the fire upon the altar shall be burning in it; it shall not
> be put out: and the priest shall burn wood on it every morn-
> ing, and lay the burnt offering in order upon it; and he shall
> burn thereon the fat of the peace offerings. The fire shall ever be
> burning upon the altar; it shall never go out.*
>
> —*Leviticus 6:12-13*

Wood represents your humanity. Burning wood on the altar
every morning means the man offers himself to God every day,
not a carnal self, because that is unacceptable to God, but a self
that is full of the fire of the Holy Ghost. Man's role as the bread
winner, the financial provider of the home, is very important, but
not to the exclusion of his responsibility as priest.

Some men feel a sense of gratification and accomplishment
about being a good provider, but when it comes to their priestly
duty to keep the fire burning, to keep the Light shining in leading
the family in devotions, they fail miserably. Work may take a great

deal of a man's time. Some men have to work two jobs to support their family, but time has to be set aside to keep the Light of God's fire shining and burning. God told Moses he would multiply the people if they spent time learning and teaching His law and His words.

When a man is not at work, his time should not be spent in his man cave watching hours of sports on cable television; he should not be isolated from his family. Men need recreation, but there has to be a balance. MAN, come out of the cave—stop acting like a caveman. Your family needs you. You were not created to be a caveman; you were created to be God's sent man. You pay bills, but what is the spiritual temperature of your house? Are you a Deuteronomy 11 man? Is your household a Deuteronomy 11 household? Is your family a Deuteronomy 11 family? Are your children Deuteronomy 11 children? What is a Deuteronomy 11 household, you may ask? Take some time and read chapter 11 of this book that represents the re-giving of God's law to His people and gauge how your life and the life of your family measure up to it.

CHAPTER 17

THE BLESSED MAN

Blessed are they that keep his testimonies,
and that seek him with the whole heart.
—*Psalm 119:2*

When the Lord decides to converse with His sent man, it will be at a time, an hour, of His choosing. In most instances it will not be an hour the natural man likes. God will call a man to reason with Him early in the morning, late at night, or in the middle of the night. He will wake you up in the middle of the night or at the crack of dawn to pray or to give you divine revelation. In those instances, the flesh wants nothing more but to hit the snooze button, roll over, and get back to sleep. You may get a few more minutes—even an hour—of sleep, but at some point, you will feel the divine pull to arise and get ready for your encounter of the God kind.

When you have a sermon to prepare, or a manuscript to write for a book based on a revelation given to you by God, it is good to have pen, paper, or some recording device near you—the Holy Spirit will release Spirit revelation to you at various times of the day or night. Early one Sunday morning before the sun rose, I arose for my morning prayer. After prayer, I sat quietly waiting to hear where the Spirit would lead me for my morning Bible reading, meditation, and study. Several verses of Psalm 1 came rushing into my spirit, mind, and soul.

The journey of a thousand miles begins with the first step. You never get a second chance to make a first impression; how something starts is key to how it develops. Anyone who has spent time reading the Psalms knows how motivating, comforting, and instructive they are. The Life Application Bible gives these vital statistics about them: *"They provide poetry for the expression of praise, worship, and confession to God. Out of the one hundred and fifty Psalms recorded in the Bible, David wrote seventy-three of them. He was profuse, prolific, and poetic in his worship of God, and in his writing."*

Since God created man to be the head of His creation, it is no wonder Psalm 1 begins with these three powerful words, *"Blessed is the man."* It is important to define the word "blessed" as it is used here. Since the word can be interpreted by many to mean a plethora of things, I'm sure everyone would agree that to be blessed is a good thing—especially when the blessing is a God thing. A man who is an atheist, an agnostic, or a secular humanist may consider himself blessed because he is financially successful, blessed because he has a beautiful family, or blessed overall because he has achieved a certain level of societal success. The "Psalm 1 Man," the term I use to describe God's blessed man, is uniquely blessed because he recognizes the fact that God is both his blessing, and is the true source of all his blessings. He knows the scripture well which states,

"The blessing of the Lord, it maketh rich, and he addeth no sorrow with it" (Prv. 10:22).

Psalm 1 gives us several key characteristics of the blessed man. So, when a man considers himself blessed, speaking of the biblical definition of the word, he should have most, if not all, the attributes listed in this Psalm. I want to focus on what it says about him in verse 2 because I believe it is the verse that sets the tone for his best life—his blessed life.

"But his delight is in the law of the Lord; and in his law doth he meditate day and night" (Ps. 1:2). The law of the Lord is synonymous with His Word, with His instructions. They produce fruitfulness when they are obeyed. The blessed man does not read and obey God's Word out of a sense of religious duty; the psalmist said it is *"his delight."* Please give me a moment to unpack this powerful word that so richly describes the blessed man's approach to the law of God.

"Delight" is the Hebrew word *chêphets* (pronounced "khay'-fets"), it means, "pleasure; hence desire; concretely, a valuable thing; hence, a matter (as something in mind): pleasant." The root word means "to favor." The blessed man takes pleasure in spending quality time in deep study and meditation of God's Word. He recognizes and greatly appreciates its value to his life. He desires the sincere milk and meat of it like a hungry and thirsty man desires great tasting, nutritious food. This is the outlook on the *rhema* word that allows him to walk in divine favor— favor with God and favor with man.

When something is good to us, we like to spend time in and around it. The law of God is better than good, so the blessed man meditates in it day and night. It speaks of commitment, it speaks of consistency, it speaks of discipline. The modern man is a very busy man. Yet the value and premium he places on the law of God motivates him to set aside the time necessary to meditate therein. He does it day and night. This is a principle which conjures up consistency. The scriptural principle of day and night, sometimes referred to as night and day as it relates to the law of God, is also seen in Joshua, chapter 1. The Psalms 1 Man can also be described as a "Joshua 1:8 Man."

This book of the law shall not depart out of thy mouth; but thou shalt meditate therein day and night, that thou mayest observe to do according to all that is written therein: for then thou shalt make thy way prosperous, and then thou shalt have good success.

—Joshua 1:8

There is a correlation between Joshua 1:8 and Psalm 1:2 in several ways: both books give the positive results of the life of the man who delights himself in the law of the Lord, the man who does not allow the book of the law to depart from his mouth. Psalm 1 uses a metaphor of the blessed man being, *"like a tree planted by the rivers of water."* The ensuing result is the blessed man being fruitful in his season. *"His leaf will not wither,"* speaks of his life not being dry and unfruitful; it speaks of him prospering in many areas of his life. It is a sharp contrast between him and the person who is described as, *"the ungodly."* They are described as chaff driven away by the wind. The way of the ungodly is not prosperous; it is a way which causes them to perish.

Both Psalm 1 and Joshua 1:8 describe a man who is all about action when it comes to the Word of God—not a man who is full of head knowledge, full of style, but severely lacking in the substance of the Word. It is a good thing to meditate in the law of God. The Joshua 1:8 Man makes his way prosperous like the Psalm 1 Man by meditating in and doing what is written in the law—in the Word. In doing so, God grants him good success. It is a great thing to observe to do all that is written in the law of the Lord.

The term "good success" is interesting since on the surface you would think success in and of itself is good.

I believe "good" is placed before "success" to stress the fact that all success is not good success. How success is gained determines whether or not it is good. A thief can have a life that has a veneer and facade of the trappings of success. He can live in a beautifully furnished mansion with exotic cars parked in his garage. He can have the latest and most expensive designer clothing due to his ill-gotten gains, but his would not be considered good success. The same thing can be said of the drug dealer, the sex trafficker, or the madam who owns a high end brothel which caters to high end clients. True good success is "God Success." The blessed man who has God Success can sleep at night; his conscience is clear. He does not have to worry about the law of man judging and locking him up because he has achieved his success through malfeasance and nefarious means—by hook or by crook. His riches come from the blessing of the Lord, so sorrow is not attached to them. His mind is not full of stress, fear, and worry; it is full of the Word of God. It is a mind that enjoys perfect peace because it is stayed on Him—perfect peace because the word of his mouth and the meditation of his heart are acceptable to God.

Both books use the word "meditate," from the Hebrew word, *hagah,* which means, "to utter, to speak." Because of the blessed man's commitment, consistency, and discipline in study and meditation of God's Word, he is able to speak it and to utter it with boldness and authority. Jesus was and is the ultimate—the consummate—Psalms 1 Man. He was the Word who became flesh and He spoke the Word when He became flesh. He spoke the Word during his wilderness temptation when He told the adversary,

"It is written, Man shall not live by bread alone, but by every word that proceedeth out of the mouth of God" (Mt. 4:4). If a man does not know what is written, he will not be able to utter or to speak what is written; hence, the blessed man's time is spent meditating in the law of the Lord, the book of the Law. When he opens his mouth, he does not speak folly or foolishness—he speaks the proceeding

Word from the mouth of God by the power of the Holy Ghost. When he does, atmospheres and spheres shift; they change.

The centurion who came to Jesus for healing for his servant understood the power of the spoken word by Jesus:

> *And when Jesus was entered into Capernaum, there came unto him a centurion, beseeching him, And saying, "Lord, my servant lieth at home sick of the palsy, grievously tormented." And Jesus saith unto him, "I will come and heal him." The centurion answered and said, "Lord, I am not worthy that thou shouldest come under my roof: but speak the word only, and my servant shall be healed. For I am a man under authority, having soldiers under me: and I say to this man, 'Go,' and he goeth; and to another, 'Come,' and he cometh; and to my servant, 'Do this,' and he doeth it." When Jesus heard it, he marvelled, and said to them that followed, "Verily I say unto you, I have not found so great faith, no, not in Israel."*
>
> *—Matthew 8:5-10*

The centurion had faith in the authority of Jesus; he had faith in the power of the words of Jesus to heal. The Word has not lost its power; when spoken by faith with authority, healing can and will take place. Adversaries will leave, albeit for a season or more, until an opportune time arises. If and when they return, don't change your modus operandi; continue to speak the Word with boldness and with authority just like Jesus Christ, the Blessed Man sent from God.

CHAPTER 18

BEHOLD, THE MAN

When Jesus stood before Pontius Pilate and the ruler uttered the words, *"Behold, the man,"* he didn't realize Yeshua was not an ordinary man. The man who stood before him was *Theanthropos*—the One in whom dwelt the fullness of the Godhead bodily. The One in whom there was neither variableness, nor shadow of turning. Pilate's wife, like most wives, was able to discern that Jesus was a just and righteous man. When Pilate was set down on the judgment seat, his wife sent unto him, saying, *"Have thou nothing to do with that just man: for I have suffered many things this day in a dream because of him"* (Mt. 27:19). Pilate himself told the people,

"I find no fault in him."

Pilate did not heed the words of his wife, and in not doing so, he condemned an innocent man to die by crucifixion. The crucifixion of Jesus of Nazareth by Governor Pontius Pilate is recorded in history. Though they were non-followers of Jesus, Pilate's wife's and Pilate's own words declared that Jesus was just and without fault—sinless in His nature, qualified to be God's sacrificial Lamb to expiate and propitiate sin. Muslims call Him a prophet. They say He was not crucified; they say someone else was crucified in His place. That theory holds no truth. The prophets of old prophesied that MASHIACH would be cut off. Judas was one of the twelve. He betrayed Him into the hands of the chief priest who turned Him over to Pontius Pilate to be examined and crucified. Pilate offered the people a choice. He told them: "'

But ye have a custom, that I should release unto you one at the passover: will ye therefore that I release unto you the King of the Jews?' Then they cried all again, saying, 'Not this man, but Barabbas.' Now Barabbas was a robber" (Jn. 18:39-40).

The chief priest knew who He was; Pilate knew who He was; the people knew who He was. The mountain of evidence shows it was Yeshua who was crucified and not another. He was not the first person to endure the debilitating, deadly effects of a Roman crucifixion, and he would not be the last. There were two male-factors crucified with him; however, the difference between Him and any other man who was crucified and was buried was He rose from the grave with all power. There is an overwhelming amount evidence of the resurrection.

The tomb in which they placed His body was empty. There were five hundred eyewitnesses who saw Him. The greatest evidence is the millions of lives that have been transformed by faith in Him—by the power of His resurrection. It's transformation which comes through what Apostle Paul called preaching Christ crucified. My Bishop, the late Reverend James Ferguson, used to give this illustration. He said, "If I have some coins in my pocket, no one can convince me they are not there." There is evidence greater than the coins that were in Bishop James' pocket; it is Christ dwelling on the throne of your heart. It is Christ in you—the hope of glory.

Pilate made the emphatic statement, *"Behold, the man."* Jesus' disciples said something emphatic about Him also. Their words were in the form of a question. Jesus was on a ship with Peter and the apostles when there arose a great tempest in the sea. The waves were so high, water was coming into the vessel. Peter and the others should have been okay because Jesus was on board, and they had seen him perform miracles before, but this time they panicked because Jesus was asleep.

"And His disciples came to Him, and awoke Him, saying, Lord, save us: we perish" (Mt. 7:25). They were so fear- and panic-stricken they couldn't form a full sentence, just the two words, *"We perish."* Christ is our Anchor. In the most egregious storms of life, the Anchor holds. Your life is like a ship sailing on tempestuous seas. The winds and the waves will be virulent; they can and will cause you to be fear- and panic-stricken like Jesus' other disciples—IF you focus on them instead of focusing on Christ who is in the storm with you. He came to save sinners because sinners could not save themselves. He has the power to save you from sin, so He definitely has the power to save you from perishing in the storm. The key is not to allow the storm to erode your faith. If you do, you will perish in the storm. Faith keeps you afloat; it keeps you buoyant.

And he saith unto them, Why are ye fearful, O ye of little faith? Then he arose, and rebuked the winds and the sea; and there was a great calm. But the men marvelled, saying, What manner of man is this, that even the winds and the sea obey him!

—Matthew 8:26-27

"Little faith," as Jesus used the term, did not mean as far as the storm was concerned. On the contrary; their *"little faith"* moved them to wake Jesus to let Him know they would perish if He did not take action. The life of every disciple will have teachable moments when he feels threatened by a storm. Will he have enough faith to rebuke the storm himself using the name of Jesus, or will he panic and say, "Lord, save me: I perish"? The "manner

of man" all men of God should be is the "Manner of Man" the disciples saw in the tempestuous storm. The One who had the power to rebuke the winds and the waves. Men sent from God have the power to rebuke in His name. Their faith can be the size of a mustard seed and/or larger, but one thing is certain—their faith is strong; it is rooted and grounded in Christ. It's the kind of faith that has the ability to calm boisterous winds and seas. God wants His sent men to demonstrate His power. When they do, unbelievers will say about them what the disciples said about Jesus. They will enquire about a man, about men, who are able to do those kinds of exploits. When they do, an opportunity will be presented to be a witness.

Another teachable moment for the disciples occurred when Jesus wanted to feed five thousand men after one of His teachings. The meeting was in a desert place so the disciples suggested Jesus send the people back to their towns and villages so they could buy food. Jesus, being the Teacher, told the disciples to give the people food to eat. I am sure they were perplexed. Why, you may ask? Well, they faced a mathematical impossibility in human terms. However, the supernatural is the source of miracles, not the natural.

The only victuals available were five coarse loaves of bread made from barley and two fish. Jesus asked the disciples to have the people sit down in groups of fifty. Fifty—the number for Jubilee; the number for Pentecost. Five for grace and two for a witness. After taking the loaves and the fish, the first thing Jesus did was look up to Heaven. Are you a man of God facing seemingly insurmountable odds, in a situation where the numbers don't add up? Is there a great need with little resources in your hands? Do what Jesus did—look up to Heaven. Jesus looked up to Heaven to teach them to look beyond their inability and look to the One who is able.

To men today, looking up to Heaven means looking to the Holy Ghost within. Look to the Kingdom of God within you. When you look up, or should I say, look in, don't do it with doubt, in panic or in fear; do it the way Jesus did. He blessed the five loaves and two fish—He gave God thanks for them. Once He looked up and gave thanks, He broke them and gave them to the disciples to give to the multitude. As he broke them, they multiplied. Broken things will multiply if your focus is on Heaven—if you are thankful. Every man was able to eat until he was full. The man sent by God has the power and the authority to bless, break, and multiply—the power and the authority to cause empty things to be filled. His focus must be on Heaven; it must be on the Kingdom; it must be on His Savior.

I implore you to reflect on the thesis laid out throughout your reading of this book, *Men Void of Light: Father, Where Are You?* In it you will find nuggets of wisdom that God has taught not only Apostle Fidel Donaldson, but all great, Godly men. Yes, we have all made our mistakes. Some of our mistakes have led to seemingly irreparable damage, but when we commit to pick up the baton, to carry the torch to be witnesses of the LIGHT, we partner with the God of Heaven to redeem His creation. Our families, our communities, our world will gain LIGHT and direction that will hopefully lead each one under our care to the true LIGHT—the Light of the World— Yahshua HaMashiach!

FIDEL'S TESTIMONY

But if any provide not for his own, and specially for those of his own house, he hath denied the faith, and is worse than an infidel.
—1 Timothy 5:8

Providing for the bills to be paid is great, but what about providing the teaching and the guidance necessary for the household to have faith in God.

Therefore, thou shalt love the Lord thy God, and keep his charge, and his statutes, and his judgments, and his commandments, alway. And know ye this day: for I speak not with your children which have not known, and which have not seen the chastisement of the Lord your God, his greatness, his mighty hand, and his stretched out arm.
—*Deuteronomy 11:1-2*

Children are not teachers—although we can learn a great deal from them. They are learners. Their brains are like sponges. They learn by watching and they learn by listening. Here is a question for every man, what are they learning from you when they watch and listen to you? For the church man, do they see you perpetrating a fraud by wearing a mask of piety in church but raising hell in your house, cussing out and even physically abusing your wife?

Is your chick on the side keeping you from spending quality time with them at eventide? What image and likeness are you presenting to them? The Image and Likeness of the God who created you, or the image and likeness of that other spirit? I used to hear a saying when I lived in Jamaica, "A man sees a man's face, but God sees his heart." Men, brothers, let us take off the masks and let us heed Polonius' token of advice to his son Laertes from Shakespeare's *Hamlet*: "

This above all: to thine own self be true / And it must follow, as the night the day / Thou canst not then be false to any man."

Most of all, men and brothers, let us be true to God Almighty.

One of my great regrets in life stems from the time I was in an English prison, separated from my wife and children. When I had freedom, I allowed myself to be an instrument of Satan instead of a priest of God who obeyed His commands. Out of great grief, great joy can be birthed if you repent and turn to God. My joy came in the place of my greatest grief because it is the place where I came to know Jesus as Lord, Savior, and King. One of the vows I made was to be a witness and a Light bearer for Him when my feet were released from the snare of incarceration.

I would begin in my household and work outward to my community and beyond. I actually started before I was released from HMP Swaleside in Kent, on the Isle of Sheppey.

Prison is a very dark place for obvious reasons, but when the eyes of my understanding were enlightened by the light of the glorious gospel of Christ, I made a conscious decision. I decided to let my Light—the Light of God's Holy Spirit that dwelt within me through confession and repentance—shine bright in a dark place. I turned my cell into a Bible study, a Deuteronomy 11 space, and I saw the transformation of the lives of other men because I dared to obey God. Many of the men around me in there were chasing the dragon (putting heroin on foil paper, heating it, then sniffing the smoke). Some smoked hashish, while others brewed hooch (moonshine) in order to get intoxicated. For me it was about shining the Light.

I didn't miss a beat when I came home. I plugged into Mount Olivet Gospel Church for teaching, training, and fellowship. I joined the men's ministry so I could watch and learn from men of God, men who were witnesses and Light bearers to their families, on their jobs, in their businesses, in their communities, and in other spheres of influence. I was coming out of a dark prison environment where the majority of men were scheming and plotting, because that is what prison will do to you if you allow it to. For protection and survival in the predatory prison environment, where the demonically controlled strong prey on the weak, inmates have to plot and scheme to get one up on the guards; not only were the inmates demonically controlled, but some guards also. Some had to plot and scheme to strike an enemy before the enemy struck them. By the grace of God, the Soldiers for Christ extricated themselves from the vicious prison cycle. They knew how to pray so they didn't become someone else's prey.

I went with a ministry team from my church to witness and bear Light at a drug and alcohol rehab center in my neighborhood; I went with another team to the notorious Rikers Island prison to do the same thing. More importantly, I kept my vow to God to be the priest of my home, to put wood on the fire every morning so the Light never went out—to allow the Holy Ghost to shine, shine, shine His Light by teaching my wife and children. Money was tight, but the gospel was right. I hit some bumps in the road, but I refused to turn back. I didn't want my two sons to be cut off like Hophni and Phinehas, whose father Eli did not discipline them in the fear and the reverence of the LORD. *"His sons made themselves vile, and he restrained them not"* (1 Sm. 3:13). I certainly did not want to be like Eli whose eyes waxed dim, and the lamp, the Light of the Lord, went out in the temple. I wanted my house to be a Deuteronomy 11 house and not the house of Eli.

I refused to look back because I was a man sent from God to be a witness of the Light.

NOTES

LIGHT BEARERS

Life Application Bible, Tyndale House Publishers, Inc. (Wheaton Illinois, 1986), 5 Sproul, 121.

For Speaking Engagements
Book Signings
Appearances, and Interviews

CONTACT

Fidel Donaldson Ministries
904-881-1886
Fidel_donaldson@yahoo.com

~

Additional Books by the Author
Diamond In the Rough
Don't Birth An Ishmael in the Waiting Room
From the Pit to the Prison to the Palace
Great Women
In he Kings Prison: A Journey of Divine Freedom
It's Time to Come Out of Lodebar
Mercy and the Sufficiency of Grace
Midnight
Perceive and Receive
Praise Worship and the Spirit of Prophecy
The Power of Persistent Prayer

BIBLIOGRAPHY

Sproul, R.C. (1995). *The Character of God: Discovering the God Who Is*. Servant Publications.